CHRISTINE S

G.O.A.T.

12 FAMOUS MATCHES FOR CANADA

● ● ●

THE G.O.A.T. — 12 FAMOUS MATCHES FOR CANADA

FOOTBALLMEDIA / BY RICHARD SCOTT
COPYRIGHT © 2023 UP NORTH PRODUCTIONS.
NO REPRODUCTION WITHOUT PERMISSION.
ALL RIGHTS RESERVED.

PUBLISHED IN CANADA BY:
UP NORTH PRODUCTIONS
1995 INDIAN CREEK ROAD
LIMOGES, ON   K0A 2M0
BOOKS@FOOTBALLMEDIA.CA

COVER DESIGN BY GRIFFIN SCOTT
PHOTO CREDITS PAGE 140

12 FAMOUS MATCHES FOR CANADA

CHRISTINE SINCLAIR THE G.O.A.T.

CANADA'S CAPTAIN EVERYTHING	5
FIRST FIFA WORLD CUP GOAL	11
OLYMPIC GAMES QUARTERFINALS	19
CONCACAF CHAMPIONSHIP WINNER	29
UM GOLAÇO DA SINCLAIR	37
THAT FREE KICK IN BERLIN	45
PAN AMERICAN GAMES GOLD MEDAL	53
SINCLAIR SENDS CANADA TO LONDON 2012	61
THE HAT TRICK AT OLD TRAFFORD	67
PENALTY WINNER AT HOME FIFA WORLD CUP	79
WONDER GOAL WINS OLYMPIC TICKET	87
BACK-TO-BACK BRONZE MEDALS	95
SINCLAIR WINS AN OLYMPIC GOLD MEDAL	103
THE GREATEST GOALSCORER OF ALL TIME	113
CHRISTINE SINCLAIR GOALS RECORD	123
CHRISTINE SINCLAIR HONOURS LIST	137

· · ·

12

CANADA'S CAPTAIN EVERYTHING

CHRISTINE SINCLAIR, O.C.
OLYMPIC CHAMPION
PROFESSIONAL FOOTBALL CHAMPION
WORLD RECORD HOLDER

Canada's Captain Everything

Christine Sinclair is an Olympic champion, a Concacaf champion, and a Pan American Games champion. She is a professional club champion, a Canadian athlete of the year, and a recipient of The Best FIFA Special Award. She is also an Officer of the Order of Canada, one of the highest awards of merit for a Canadian.

As an international goalscorer, she is simply The Greatest of All Time.

Yet what would a book about Christine Sinclair be without the story of her teammates and Canada Soccer's Women's National Team. While she has scored more international goals than any other player in the history of football, she thrives first and foremost as a teammate.

Beyond the pitch, Sinclair and her teammates take great responsibility as role models and as an inspiration to the next generation.

"My entire career has been about inspiring the next generation," said Sinclair. "I think (with London 2012) that was our rallying cry. I am now teammates with players that tell me they remember watching (those Games) and that's when they decided they wanted to play for Canada.

"Now it's only going to be bigger. That next generation of young kids that watched Canada win Gold in Tokyo will be on the National Team and hopefully it will bring more and more opportunities for the young kids."

As a tribute to Canada's number 12 and her journey to an Olympic Gold Medal, we have picked 12 of her most famous international matches for Canada. We've also featured short player vignettes for 25 of her Canada teammates plus six of her legendary world opponents.

Sinclair's 12 famous matches for Canada

From FIFA World Cups and Olympic Tournaments to the Concacaf Championship and Pan American Games, we've highlighted some of Sinclair's biggest moments as an international footballer. There is the golaço at São Paulo, the free kick at Berlin, the hat trick at Old Trafford, and the wonder goal in Olympic Qualifiers.

The bigger the moment, the better Sinclair played for Canada. There's her title-winning goal against Mexico in Mexico for the 2010 Concacaf Championship, the hometown brace that booked Canada's ticket to the London 2012 Olympic Games, her last-minute penalty winner at Canada's home FIFA World Cup, and the match winner against Brazil in Brazil to capture back-to-back Olympic Bronze Medals.

As for the goals, you will note that while Sinclair scored more goals for Canada in her first decade, we've featured far more Canada goals from her second decade. With full apologies to those first 10 years, while her first decade may have established her as a superstar, her second decade immortalised her as a legend of the game.

From 2000 to 2009, she scored 99 international goals in 132 matches (75% goalscoring rate) and helped Canada win 60 matches (45% win rate). Canada finished fourth at the FIFA World Cup in 2003 and reached the Olympic Quarterfinals in 2008.

From 2010 to 2019, she scored 84 international goals in 157 matches (53.5% goalscoring rate) and helped Canada win 95 matches (60.5% win rate). Canada won the Concacaf Championship in 2010, the Pan American Games in 2011, and back-to-back Olympic Bronze Medals in 2012 and 2016. She was also named Canada's Player of the Decade.

Pretty impressive, but not nearly as enduring as the one accolade she picked up in her third decade: an Olympic Gold Medal with her Canada teammates.

So even when Sinclair didn't score for Canada, she was as dangerous a footballer the game has ever seen. Case in point: down a goal in that Olympic Gold Medal Final, she drew the penalty that allowed Canada to equalise against Sweden. It was but a split moment, but it was the moment that changed the course of the match for Canada.

"The Olympic Gold Medal for me still tops everything that I have achieved in my career just because it is something that I have been striving for since I was that four-year old girl learning to kick a soccer ball."

Christine Sinclair Legacy

"You would never know from speaking to her, or working with her, that she's the world's all-time leading goalscorer," said Canada Head Coach Bev Priestman after the Olympic Games in 2021. "She won her 300th cap in our opening match at the Olympics and didn't want a word spoken about it because she didn't want a distraction for the team. That kind of attitude isn't always the norm in players, but what she and the others bring to the team on a human level is amazing."

There are a number of legacies to which Christine Sinclair will be attributed after her playing career, but scoring goals probably doesn't crack the top-five list.

She was a winner and she showed up best in the big moments. She was a proud and genuine Canadian. She was a selfless teammate and incredible leader. She had an unparalleled understanding of the game and was most often the smartest player on the pitch. Her preparation and training have been second to none which allowed her to have an exceptionally long and successful career.

"I go about every day trying to be the best Canadian that I can in my own way," said Sinclair.

Through everything that she has done and continues to do on and off the pitch, she remains an inspiration to millions of people in Canada and around the world.

"She's such a great Canadian and this is reflected in her leadership of our team, not only in the way that she can inspire her teammates, but also in the way that she can inspire all Canadians," said former Head Coach John Herdman in 2016.

So yeah, Christine Sinclair is a pretty good goalscorer, but she is first and foremost an incredible human being.

"For me, (greatness) has nothing to do with the (international goals) record," said Sinclair. "It's just to have young girls be able to dream to play professionally or represent their country, win Olympic medals and not be thought of as strange or weird... to be able to inspire young girls to pursue their crazy, wild dreams, that's pretty cool."

CANADIAN LEGEND • GERI DONNELLY

An honoured member of the Canada Soccer Hall of Fame, Geri Donnelly left international football as Canada's all-time leader in appearances, a record passed by Charmaine Hooper in 2001 (after which Hooper's record was passed by Christine Sinclair in 2010). An original member of Canada Soccer's Women's National Team in 1986 (and the team's first-ever goal-scorer), Donnelly represented Canada at two FIFA World Cups and won a Concacaf Championship in 1998. She was a two-time Canada Soccer Player of the Year after the award was introduced for women's footballers in 1994. She was a recipient of Canada Soccer's Aubrey Sanford Meritorious Service Award in 2002.

In all, Donnelly won four Concacaf medals in the 1990s (one Gold, two Silver, one Bronze). Before the first FIFA World Cup, she helped Canada finish in fifth place at the 1987 World Invitational Tournament in Chinese Taipei and then in sixth place at the 1988 Women's International Tournament in China.

Donnelly, who hung up her boots at age 43 in 2009, played her last match for Canada at the FIFA World Cup in 1999. She took part in her last National Team camp in 2000, the same year in which Christine Sinclair got her first call up by new Head Coach Even Pellerud.

Alongside Donnelly, 16 other honoured members from the Canada Soccer Hall of Fame played their last international match before Sinclair's debut in March 2000. That group features: goalkeepers Carla Chin Baker and Sue Simon; centre backs and fullbacks Sue Brand, Tracy David, Janine (Wood) Helland, Janet Lemieux, Luce Mongrain, and Cathy Ross; and midfielders/forwards Connie Cant, Annie Caron, Angela Kelly, Joan McEachern, Suzanne Muir, Michelle Ring, Carrie Serwetnyk, and Helen Stoumbos.

CANADIAN LEGEND • SILVANA BURTINI

An honoured member of the Canada Soccer Hall of Fame, Silvana Burtini retired from Canada in 2003 ranked third in all-time international goals and appearances. She represented Canada at three FIFA World Cups including a fourth-place finish in 2003. She also won a Concacaf Championship and was Canada's Player of the Year in 1998.

Burtini won four Concacaf medals (one Gold, two Silver, one Bronze) and was a two-time Top Scorer at the Concacaf Championship (1994 and 1998). Before the first FIFA World Cup, she helped Canada finish in sixth place at the 1988 Women's International Tournament in China.

From 2000 to 2003, Burtini and Sinclair were on the pitch together 31 times for Canada. When they were both on the pitch at the same time, Sinclair scored 21 goals and Burtini scored eight goals.

GREATEST OF ALL TIME

FIRST FIFA WORLD CUP GOAL

FIFA WORLD CUP USA 2003
COLUMBUS, OHIO, USA
SATURDAY 20 SEPTEMBER 2003
CREW STADIUM (16,409 SPECTATORS)

Sinclair's first FIFA World Cup goal

It took Christine Sinclair less than five minutes to score her first career FIFA World Cup goal in the opening match at Columbus in 2003. It was the 1-0 goal, albeit in a 4-1 loss, to the eventual FIFA World Cup champions Germany who never looked back after scoring their first goal on a penalty in the 39th minute. Sinclair scored her historic goal on a header from a Kristina Kiss free kick towards the back post in the fourth minute.

Before the end of the first half, Bettina Wiegmann scored the 1-1 equaliser on a penalty. Across the second half, Stefanie Gottschlich, Birgit Prinz and Kerstin Garefrekes put the match out of reach for the 4-1 victory. Maren Meinert, who recorded two assists, also hit the crossbar in the 90th minute when the score was still 3-1.

FIFA World Cup USA 2003

The FIFA World Cup was played in the United States for the second time in a row, although it was originally scheduled for China until there was an outbreak of SARS in that region in early 2003. In May, FIFA moved the

---

CANADIAN LEGEND • CHARMAINE HOOPER

An honoured member of the Canada Soccer Hall of Fame as well as Canada's Sports Hall of Fame, forward Charmaine Hooper retired as Canada's all-time international leader in goals and appearances, both records since passed. An original member of Canada Soccer's Women's National Team in 1986, she represented Canada at three FIFA World Cups and also won a Concacaf Championship in 1998. She was a four-time Canada Soccer Player of the Year after the award was introduced for women's footballers in 1994.

Along with a fourth-place finish at the 2003 FIFA World Cup, she won six Concacaf medals from 1991 to 2004 (one Gold, three Silver and two Bronze). She also helped Canada finish in fifth place at the 1987 World Invitational Tournament in Chinese Taipei. In 2003 in the build up to the FIFA World Cup, she helped Canada set a program record with a 10-match undefeated streak.

From 2000 to 2006, Hooper and Sinclair were on the pitch together 59 times for Canada. When they were both on the pitch at the same time, Hooper scored 33 goals and Sinclair scored 31 goals.

FIFA World Cup out of China (they were awarded the next tournament in 2007) and then named USA as the hosts with less than four months to prepare for the 2003 tournament. Canada's opening match on Saturday 20 September was played in front of 16,409 fans at Crew Stadium in Columbus (almost 75% capacity).

With a shortfall of defenders ahead of the FIFA World Cup, Canada's Head Coach Even Pellerud turned the team's all-time goalscoring leader Charmaine Hooper into a central defender. Hooper, an original member of the Women's National Team since 1986, was also the oldest player in the squad at age 35. So Pellerud's new front line featured three players 22 years or younger: Sinclair (20), Christine Latham (22), and Kara Lang (16). Along with Lang, Canada's starting lineup against Germany also featured teenagers Tanya Dennis, Brittany Timko and Diana Matheson.

Stadium, referees and lineups

COLUMBUS, OHIO, USA - Saturday 20 September 2003 at Crew Stadium (16,409 spectators). **REFEREES** - Im Eun Ju (KOR), Choi Soo Jin (KOR), Hong Kum Nyo (KOR), Sandra Hunt (USA).
CANADA - 1 GK Karina LeBlanc; 18 Tanya Dennis, 6 Sharolta Nonen, 10 Charmaine Hooper captain, 16 Brittany Timko, 5 Andrea Neil, 8 Kristina Kiss, 13 Diana Matheson, 15 Kara Lang (9 Rhian Wilkinson HT), 2 Christine Latham, 12 Christine Sinclair. Coach: Even Pellerud. Did not feature: 19 Erin McLeod, 20 Tara Swiatek, 3 Linda Consolante, 4 Sasha Andrews, 7 Isabelle Morneau, 11 Randee Hermus (Inj.), 14 Carmelina Moscato, 17 Silvana Burtini.
GERMANY - 1 GK Silke Rottenberg; 2 Kerstin Stiegemann, 3 Linda Bresonik, 17 Ariane Hingst (4 Nia Kuenzer 65'), 13 Sandra Minnert, 19 Stefanie Gottschlich, 5 Steffi Jones, 10 Bettina Wiegmann captain, 6 Renate Ringor (18 Kerstin Garefrekes 73'), 14 Maren Meinert, 9 Birgit Prinz. Coach: Tina Theune-Mayer. Did not feature: 15 GK Nadine Angerer, 4 Nia Künzer, 7 Pia Wunderlich, 8 Sandra Smisek, 11 Martina Müller, 12 Sonja Fuss, 16 Viola Odebrecht, 20 Conny Pohlers.

Sinclair the teen scoring machine

Christine Sinclair had already scored 25 international goals in 35 matches with the full National Team before she took part in the first FIFA youth tournament in 2002. She had also scored 17 goals in just 13 youth international matches, which included a nine-match tour across Canada to help promote the inaugural FIFA U-19 Women's World Championship Canada 2002.

Right from the get go, Sinclair was the star of the tournament. It took her less than 15 minutes to score her first goal in the opener against Denmark, a 3-2 come-from-behind victory in front of more than 21,000 fans at Commonwealth Stadium in Edmonton. It was the largest crowd in front of which Sinclair had ever played for Canada, at either the international "A" or youth level. After she scored another two goals against Japan and then another two after that against Nigeria to wrap up the group phase, Sinclair scored five goals to eliminate England in the tournament Quarterfinals.

"It was an excellent game for us," mused the teen captain Sinclair after the Quarterfinals. "It was one of those games where almost every chance I had went into the net. It was just one of those days and it feels great to be going into the Semifinals."

Against England, Sinclair started the scoring less than five minutes after kickoff, then wrapped it up with the 6-2 goal shortly before the final whistle. Across the match, she scored her first goal on a header at the near post on a Carmelina Moscato corner kick, her second goal with her right foot from inside the box, her third goal early in the second half with her left foot, her fourth goal again with her right foot from inside the box now in the 91st minute, and finally her fifth goal just a couple of minutes later with her left foot on a rebound.

From Sinclair's five-goal performance, the excitement and the crowds just exploded for Canada's last two matches of the tournament. After attendance dipped below 20,000 for Canada's midweek matches in the group phase, there were 23,595 fans in attendance for their Sunday afternoon Quarterfinals. That was again the biggest crowd in front of which Sinclair, or any of her teammates, had ever played for Canada. Four days later, the attendance was 37,194 for the Thursday Semifinals against Brazil, then it went up to 47,784 for the Sunday afternoon Final against USA.

While Sinclair technically didn't score in the last two matches of the tournament, she did score on her kick from the penalty mark in the Semifinals against Brazil. Canada won 4-3 on kicks after a 1-1 draw, the first-ever international meeting between Sinclair and future six-time World Player of the Year Marta. The 16-year old Brazilian star scored the 1-1 equaliser in the second half, but then after extra time had her kick stopped by goalkeeper Erin McLeod. Canada won 4-3 on kicks and advanced to an all-North American dream Final against rivals USA.

"They came out and put everything into every tackle," said Sinclair of the Brazil match. "That's how Canada plays, but it was the first time we ever played a team that was willing to match us."

In the FIFA Final, Canada had the support of more than 47,000 fans, the biggest attendance of any soccer match hosted in Canada in eight years *(since 1994 when Canada Soccer's Men's National Team held the soon-to-be-crowned FIFA World Cup champions Brazil to a 1-1 draw at Edmonton)*. On this day, every time Sinclair touched the ball or made a darting run towards the penalty area, the crowd roared her forward. It was almost enough as Canada created some incredible chances in the second half, especially in the five minutes before the hour mark when Moscato hit the top of the crossbar on a corner kick and Katie Thorlakson hit the post from a Sinclair pass.

Then in the 90th minute, Sinclair somehow got past two defenders and created her own space inside the penalty area for the most glorious of chances that could have sealed a perfect ending for the Canadians. Her shot, however, somehow went over the crossbar.

The amazing Christine Sinclair

From the FIFA U-19 World Championship where she won both the FIFA Golden Ball (best player) and FIFA Golden Shoe (top scorer), Sinclair was quickly becoming a household name across Canada. In the next year before the FIFA World Cup USA 2003, she scored another 15 international goals, was Concacaf's joint top scorer at the Gold Cup, won the College Cup in her first year at the University of Portland, finished fourth in voting for Canada's 2002 Female Athlete of the Year award, and helped Canada set a program record with a 10-match undefeated streak from May to September leading into the 2003 FIFA World Cup. She even fought off a bout with mononucleosis in June and July.

After sitting out two months in between matches, Sinclair came back to score the opening goal of a 1-1 draw with Ghana at Seattle on Saturday 16 August, now just over a month away from the opening match at the FIFA World Cup. She followed up with a goal and two assists in a 8-0 win over Mexico on Sunday 31 August, also her first match back at Commonwealth Stadium since the FIFA U-19 World Championship. The Sunday afternoon friendly at Edmonton drew 29,953 spectators, a new attendance record for the Women's National Team at home in Canada.

From there, she made her 50th international "A" appearance four days later at sold-out Swangard Stadium in her hometown Burnaby (a 6-0 win over Mexico in front of 6,210 fans) and then came off the bench 10 days later in front of another capacity crowd at Richardson Stadium in Kingston, Ontario (a 2-0 win over Australia in front of 10,068 fans).

Said 20-year old Sinclair in the Kingston *Whig-Standard* before the 2003 FIFA World Cup, "I'm really excited. It's a tournament you wait your life to play in."

Sinclair's first FIFA World Cup

Sinclair was just 16 years old when she attended the 1999 FIFA World Cup as a fan in Portland, Oregon. When the tournament wrapped up on Saturday 10 July, she watched American Brandi Chastain score the winning kick back home in British Columbia.

"I was back home in Vancouver and I was just in awe (because) USA did an incredible job hosting it," said Sinclair years later before Canada hosted the FIFA World Cup in 2015. "It was the first time that women's soccer was on the map. I remember watching the games and it was in that moment that I decided that I'm going to play in the next one of these (in 2003) and I did."

Christine Sinclair played in every minute of every match in her first FIFA World Cup, with matches played at Columbus, Foxborough (near

CANADIAN LEGEND • BRITTANY TIMKO

Brittany Timko was one of seven players from Canada's 2003 FIFA World Cup team that won an Olympic Bronze Medal just nine years later at London 2012. She was also one of just four players that went from the FIFA U-19 World Championship in 2002 to the FIFA World Cup in 2003 and then an Olympic Bronze Medal in 2012.

An honoured member of the Canada Soccer Hall of Fame, she represented Canada at three FIFA World Cups and two Olympic Games. She won five Concacaf medals, but she missed the 2010 Concacaf Championship through injury. She left international football in 2014 ranked fourth all time in Canada appearances.

From 2002 to 2014, Timko and Sinclair were on the pitch together 115 times for Canada. Timko played as a forward, midfielder and fullback for Canada. Timko and Sinclair were also teammates at Vancouver Whitecaps FC where they won the 2006 USL W-League Championship.

At the youth level after Sinclair won the Golden Boot at the FIFA U-19 World Championship Canada 2002, Timko won the same award two years later at Thailand 2004.

Boston), Portland, and Carson (near Los Angeles). After their initial loss to Germany, they won back-to-back matches in the group phase, beat the previous FIFA World Cup runners up China PR in the Quarterfinals, then lost in the last 15 minutes of the Semifinals to 2003 runners up Sweden. They lost to the Americans in the Match for Third Place six days later on Saturday 11 October.

Sinclair scored three goals in her first FIFA World Cup: one against Germany, one against Japan, and one against USA. She also recorded an assist in the 3-1 win over Japan and hit the goal post in the 3-1 loss to the United States.

Incidentally, she scored at Columbus, Foxborough and Carson, but missed scoring a goal at Portland.

Her first FIFA World Cup goal was scored on a jumping header from less than seven yards out on the free kick by teammate Kiss. She scored the goal in the fourth minute for a 1-0 lead against Germany's Silke Rottenberg.

Her second FIFA World Cup goal was scored a week later against future FIFA World Cup champions Japan, although on this day Canada were the dominant side for a 3-1 victory. Sinclair scored the 2-1 match winner in the 49th minute against Nozomi Yamago on a jumping header from less than seven yards out. This time, the cross came from a Brittany Timko corner kick on the left side.

On her third FIFA World Cup goal, Sinclair was sent through on a breakaway by teammate Christine Latham for the 1-1 equaliser in the 38th minute against USA. Sinclair followed the ball into the 18-yard box and one-timed her low, right-footed shot past American goalkeeper Briana Scurry.

GREATEST OF ALL TIME

OLYMPIC QUARTER-FINALS

BEIJING 2008 OLYMPIC GAMES
SHANGHAI, CHINA
FRIDAY 15 AUGUST 2008
SHANGHAI STADIUM (26,129 SPECTATORS)

Olympic Quarterfinals at Beijing 2008

In an epic Olympic Quarterfinals match against their rivals USA that was interrupted by lightning at Shanghai, Christine Sinclair scored the 1-1 equaliser in the (official) 30th minute from a well driven, right-footed shot from distance. The play started with a harmless Heather Mitts throw in on the right side, but Canadian midfielder Clare Rustad caused the turnover at Carli Lloyd's feet and the ball rolled perfectly to Sinclair who smashed it past the diving American goalkeeper Hope Solo.

It was a momentous moment for the Canadians and Sinclair was quick to her celebration, first with her arms up in the air, then a little clap and at last a finger pointed to the air before she was mobbed by her teammates. After neither side scored again for more than an hour, Canada lost the match 2-1 in extra time on a header scored by substitute Natasha Kai in the 101st minute.

Beijing 2008 Olympic Games

This was Canada's first participation in the Women's Olympic Football Tournament and they reached the knockout phase by finishing in third place in their group after a win, a draw and a loss. Sinclair scored her first career Olympic goal in the second group match against the hosts China PR in front of 52,600 spectators, the largest crowd in front of which Canada Soccer's Women's National Team had ever played.

Coach Pellerud featured a relatively unchanged lineup throughout the Olympic Games, with notably the same group of 10 players starting all four matches. Only forward Melissa Tancredi missed one start in the group phase because of an injury. After opening the tournament with a 2-1 win over Argentina on goals by Candace Chapman and Kara Lang, Sinclair scored her first Olympic goal in the 1-1 draw with China PR at the Tianjin Olympic Sports Center Stadium on Saturday 9 August. Three days later, Canada qualified for the Olympic Quarterfinals despite a 2-1 loss to Sweden at the Workers' Stadium in Beijing (with only 5,112 fans in attendance). Tancredi scored the last goal of the group phase from an Amy Walsh cross just three minutes after the hour mark.

Stadium, referees and lineups

SHANGHAI, CHINA - Friday 15 August 2008 at Shanghai Stadium (26,129 spectators)
REFEREES - Jenny Palmqvist (SWE); Helen Karo (SWE); Hege Steinlund (NOR); Estela Alvarez (ARG).

CANADA - 18 GK Erin McLeod Injured (1 GK Karina LeBlanc 19'); 7 Rhian Wilkinson, 9 Candace Chapman, 10 Martina Franko, 3 Emily Zurrer, 15 Kara Lang, 6 Sophie Schmidt, 8 Diana Matheson, 4 Clare Rustad, 14 Melissa Tancredi (17 Brittany Timko HT later injured, 16 Jonelle Filigno 90'), 12 Christine Sinclair captain. Coach: Even Pellerud. Did not feature: 2 Jodi-Ann Robinson, 5 Robyn Gayle, 11 Randee Hermus, 13 Amy Walsh.

USA - 1 Hope Solo; 2 Heather Mitts, 3 Christie Rampone captain, 15 Kate Markgraf, 17 Lori Chalupny, 9 Heather O'Reilly (6 Natasha Kai 91'), 11 Carli Lloyd, 7 Shannon Boxx, 5 Lindsay Tarpley (13 Tobin Heath 82'), 16 Angela Hucles, 8 Amy Rodriguez (12 Lauren Cheney 109'). Coach: Pia Sundhage. Did not feature: 18 GK Nicole Barnhart, 4 Rachel Buehler, 14 Stephanie Cox, 10 Aly Wagner.

From FIFA World Cups to the Olympic Games

From finishing fourth overall at the FIFA World Cup in 2003, Canada missed the 2004 Olympic Games after they were eliminated by Mexico at the Concacaf Qualifiers in Costa Rica. On Wednesday 3 March, Canada lost 2-1 after a high noon kickoff at the Estadio Nacional in San José on a pair of goals by Maribel Domínguez.

After the disappointment of 2004, it was two years before Sinclair had a chance to help Canada qualify for the FIFA World Cup in 2007. At the 2006 Concacaf Gold Cup, she scored the match winner in the 40th minute then added an assist and another goal in the second half en route to a 4-0 win over Jamaica. Four days later on Sunday 26 November, Canada finished in second place after a 2-1 loss to the Americans on Kristine Lilly's added-time penalty winner in extra time. In the words of ejected coach Even Pellerud, it was a "doubtful" penalty called by referee Virginia Tovar.

In 2007, Canada won a Bronze Medal at the Pan American Games in Brazil where Sinclair set Canada's all-time record for international goals. She scored a hat trick in the opening 7-0 win over Uruguay, with her first of the match the record-breaking 72nd goal to surpass former captain Charmaine Hooper. Sinclair scored eight goals in five matches en route to a third-place finish, but she did not score in Brazil's 7-0 demolishing that kept Canada out of the Gold Medal Final. In the last match, Sinclair scored the opening goal in the 2-1 win over Mexico to capture the Bronze Medal.

Less than two months after the Pan American Games, Sinclair scored three goals in three matches at the FIFA World Cup in China, but Canada were eliminated on an added time winner by Cheryl Salisbury after Canada failed to clear the ball from in front of their net. Sinclair had scored the 2-1 go-ahead goal in the 85th minute which should have sent Canada through to the Quarterfinals, but instead Australia spoiled Canada's party and sent them packing at the end of the night.

CANADA QUALIFY FOR THE OLYMPIC GAMES

Just over half a year after the 2007 FIFA World Cup, Canada were in Juárez, Coahuila for the 2008 Concacaf Olympic Qualifiers. After back-to-back wins against Trinidad and Tobago and Costa Rica, they met hosts Mexico in the Concacaf Semifinals with a spot for the Olympic Games on the line. The match was played on a Wednesday night with a packed crowd of 19,850 Mexican fans at the Estadio Olímpico Benito Juárez.

Unlike four years earlier, there was no mistake this time from the Canadians as the qualified for the Olympic Games for the first time in program history. In the 25th minute, Tancredi scored the only goal on a breakaway after she picked up a loose ball when Rubí Sandoval slipped to the ground.

Three days after Canada qualified for the Olympic Games, they pushed USA to the limit in the Concacaf Final, now with only 4,115 fans in attendance. The match was scoreless through 90 minutes, then Carli Lloyd scored the opener in the 109th minute. Tancredi, however, equalised in the 116th minute. On kicks from the penalty mark, the two sides went toe to toe for seven rounds before USA walked off the 6-5 winners from Nicole Barnhart's final save.

The Canada-USA football rivalry

By the time Canada faced USA at the Olympic Games in 2008, Christine Sinclair had already faced the Americans 23 times in nine seasons at the international "A" level (not counting the youth teams). There were a couple of wins in her first two years, but otherwise the Americans dominated the rivalry with 17 wins and four draws. In 2008, the two sides met each other a record five times and the Americans outscored the Canadians 14-2.

While that 2008 record included a couple of blow outs, the scores were often close when the stakes were at their highest. The score was 1-1 in the Final of the Concacaf Olympic Qualifiers (USA won 6-5 on kicks), 1-0 in the Peace Queen Cup Final, and 2-1 after extra time in that famous Olympic Quarterfinals match at Shanghai Stadium.

Including the Beijing 2008 Olympic Games, Sinclair scored in eight of her first 24 international matches against the United States, including goals in both the 2000 and 2001 victories (a 3-1 win at Columbus and then a 3-0 win at the 2001 Algarve Cup).

In other matches against the U.S., she scored: Canada's only goal in a 9-1 loss down under at the 2000 Pacific Cup in Australia (her first international goal against the Americans); the opening goal in a blowout 6-1 loss at Washington before the 2003 FIFA World Cup; the 1-1 goal in a 3-1 loss in the Match for 3rd Place at the 2003 FIFA World Cup; and a second-half goal in a 6-2 loss near Dallas in a 2007 international friendly.

Sinclair also scored the 2-2 equaliser in a 2001 draw against the Americans at Varsity Stadium in Toronto, which was also her first-ever home international match for Canada. Second-half substitute Tiffeny Milbrett scored the 2-1 go-ahead goal on a right-footed strike from distance in the 57th minute, but then Sinclair tied it up just 82 seconds later after a clearance attempt by goalkeeper Nicole Barnhart.

In that 58th minute sequence, Isabelle Morneau won the turnover and played it to Silvana Burtini who then sprung Sinclair on the run down the left side of the pitch. Sinclair's cross into the box was miss cleared by centre back Catherine Reddick into the air, Barnhart barely punch it away from Latham's potential header, and the ball fell into the path of Sinclair who one-timed it into the back of the net to the delight of the 9,023 Canadian fans.

When Canada faced the United States at the 2008 Olympic Games, Sinclair was a seasoned veteran with 94 career international goals.

While Canada were coming off a ninth-place finish at the most recent FIFA World Cup in China, the Americans were coming off back-to-back third-place finishes at the 2003 and 2007 FIFA World Cups and they were the reigning Olympic champions from 2004.

"It's so exciting," said Sinclair to Terry Jones at the *Edmonton Sun* before the Olympic Quarterfinals. "We love to play them. It's a huge rivalry. We get excited to play them any time, but now we get to play them in the Olympics.

"The U.S. is probably the best team in the world, but we know we can play with them."

Sinclair scores her first Olympic goal at Tianjin

In the group stage against China PR, Sinclair scored her first Olympic goal on a right-footed shot from inside the box just a moment after Kara Lang chipped her through with a brilliant pass over top centre back Li Jie. Sinclair's opener was scored in the 34th minute, but the 1-0 lead lasted less than two minutes before Xu Yuan scored the 1-1 equaliser.

On the sequence that led to the Canada's 1-0 goal, goalkeeper Zhang Yanru's kick was headed back by Sophie Schmidt, right back Liu Huana miss cleared with her own header right to the chest of Lang, and then from Lang's chip pass over Li it was Sinclair who ran into the box and hit the bouncing ball past Zhang.

Champs beat Canada in extra time

In the Friday night Olympic Quarterfinals at Shanghai Stadium, the Americans took a 1-0 lead in the 13th minute on a goal by Angela Hucles in the driving rain. Goalkeeper Erin McLeod dove to push away a Heather O'Reilly header, but the ball fell into the path of Hucles at the back post who made no mistake with her right foot. On the play, McLeod was injured and eventually could not continue. She was replaced by Karina LeBlanc less than seven minutes later.

Just a minute after LeBlanc entered in the match, referee Jenny Palmqvist sent both teams inside for more than an hour on account of lightning. It was about 10 minutes after the match resumed that Sinclair scored the 1-1 equaliser in the 30th minute of her 125th career international match.

In the rain with the score tied, there were chances, but nothing special enough to break the deadlock. Hucles probably could have had a hat trick while Amy Rodriguez had a shot pushed away by LeBlanc less than a minute before extra time. Sinclair had Canada's best chance on a low shot from distance that was easily saved by Solo in the 78th minute.

The 2-1 winner was scored in extra time in the 101st minute on the Kai header from a Shannon Boxx cross into the six-yard box. Canada tried for about 20 minutes to get an equaliser, but the score remained unchanged and their Olympic journey was over.

Three days later in the Olympic Semifinals, USA won 4-2 over Japan while Brazil won 4-1 over the FIFA World Cup champions Germany. Another three days later on 21 August, the Americans won their third Olympic Gold Medal with a 1-0 win on a Carli Lloyd goal in extra time.

Sinclair's technique is outstanding

"What a strike," said Jason deVos on CBC, the Canadian broadcaster for the 2008 Olympic Games. "Christine Sinclair smashes the ball from 25 yards and Hope Solo is left with no chance."

On American television, former FIFA World Cup champion and NBC colour commentator Brandi Chastain couldn't say enough about Sinclair's prowess and skill.

"I liken Christine Sinclair to the embers in the fire that are just very hot but you can't tell, (then) all of a sudden one poke to them and it's just a blaze," said Chastain, who in 2009 became Sinclair's teammate at FC Gold Pride in the WPS. "That's the type of player that she is: very dangerous and she can be hot in an instant."

"What you saw in her technique is outstanding (because she's) very compact, it comes from her hips (which are) very tight and locked all the way down through her ankle. She has a follow through and she lands on her kicking foot (while her) head is very still. She's what I call a slow twitcher. You don't see her making these darting dashing things in and out of players, but she can pick up speed over space (and) she just has incredible control in shooting. It's marvelous to watch."

"She's actually similar to Carli Lloyd in that way who has the ability to hit the ball with some pace and some power."

Asked to compare Sinclair to Abby Wambach, Chastain said, "I think they are both similar, they are both big in stature, they do have good pace over distance (and) they are technically gifted with both feet. I think Abby scores a few more fortuitous, opportunistic goals than Christine Sinclair, but I think they are both fabulous goalscorers and people who are incredibly integral to the success of their teams."

An electrifying first decade for Canada

In her first decade as an international footballer from 2000 to 2009, Sinclair scored 99 goals in 132 matches. From her first season in 2000, she became the program's youngest debutant and goalscorer at age 16, set a Canada record for goals in a season (15), and was selected Canada's Player of the Year. Just two years later in 2002, she was a FIFA World Player candidate for the first time (sixth overall) and a finalist for *The Canadian Press* Athlete of the Year (fourth overall). In 2007, she became the program's all-time leading goalscorer and broke her own Canada record for goals in a season (16).

After the Olympic Games in 2008, Sinclair was a FIFA World Player candidate for the fifth time in seven years, she won her sixth Canada Soccer Player of the Year award since 2000, and she led Canada in goalscoring for the eighth time in nine years. Through to the Olympic Quarterfinals in Shanghai, she played all nine international seasons under the leadership of coach Pellerud.

In 2009, the 25-year old Sinclair also turned pro with the FC Gold Pride for the inaugural Women's Professional Soccer season. She was drafted eighth overall in the WPS International Draft one month after the Olympic Games on 24 September 2008. She then joined her new club in March after the 2009 Cyprus Cup and made her professional debut against the Boston Breakers on Sunday 5 April. Sinclair scored six goals in 17 matches, but FC Gold Pride finished last overall in the standings (they won everything just one year later in 2010).

On the international scene in 2009 with newly-appointed coach Carolina Morace in charge, Sinclair won her seventh Player of the Year award and led Canada in goalscoring for the ninth time. In her first match of the new decade against Poland in 2010, she scored her 100th international goal and set the Canada all-time record with 133 career matches (one more than former teammate Andrea Neil, who was now an assistant coach with Morace).

CANADIAN LEGEND • RANDEE HERMUS

Randee Hermus made her Olympic debut in front of 52,600 fans at the Tianjin Olympic Sports Center Stadium in a 1-1 draw with the hosts China PR. It was also her last match for Canada in an 11-year international career in which she made the fourth-most appearances in program history.

An honoured member of the Canada Soccer Hall of Fame, Hermus represented Canada at two FIFA World Cups and won four Concacaf medals. She notably played in 46 consecutive Canada matches from 2005 to 2008, at the time a national record (broken four years later by Sophie Schmidt).

From 2000 to 2008, Hermus and Sinclair were on the pitch together 98 times for Canada. At the club level, Hermus and Sinclair were together at Whitecaps FC when they won the 2006 USL W-League Championship.

CANADIAN LEGEND • ANDREA NEIL

After 18 international seasons, Andrea Neil made her last appearance for Canada at the FIFA World Cup in 2007. A member of four FIFA World Cup teams including a fourth-place finish at USA 2003, Neil left football as Canada's all-time leader in international "A" appearances.

An honoured member of both the Canada Soccer Hall of Fame and Canada's Sports Hall of Fame, she also won five Concacaf medals from 1991 to 2006. She was the 2001 Canada Soccer Player of the Year.

From 2000 to 2007, Neil and Sinclair were on the pitch together 86 times for Canada. After her retirement, Neil's Canada record for appearances was broken by Sinclair in 2010. At the club level, Neil and Sinclair helped Whitecaps FC win the 2006 USL W-League Championship.

CANADIAN LEGEND • AMY WALSH

Amy Walsh was one of two Concacaf champions from 1998 that played for Canada at their first Women's Olympic Football Tournament 10 years later in 2008 (alongside goalkeeper Karina LeBlanc). It turned out to be Walsh's last major tournament and she recorded an assist in the 2-1 loss to Sweden.

An honoured member of the Canada Soccer Hall of Fame, Walsh also played at two FIFA World Cups and won four Concacaf medals including Gold in 1998. In all, she made 102 appearances across a 12-year career with Canada.

From 2000 to 2009, Walsh and Sinclair were on the pitch together 75 times for Canada. Walsh was notably Canada's captain when Sinclair made her international debut in 2000.

GREATEST OF ALL TIME

CONCACAF CHAMPIONSHIP WINNER

CONCACAF WORLD CUP QUALIFYING
CANCÚN, QUINTANA ROO, MEXICO
MONDAY 8 NOVEMBER 2010
ESTADIO QUINTANA ROO (16,005 SPECTATORS)

Sinclair scores Championship winner

Cool, calm, collected, captain Christine Sinclair picked up the ball and tucked it under her left arm, her right hand rested on her hip as she waited for referee Shane De Silva to sort things out. Moments earlier with 10 Mexicans defending in their box, Sophie Schmidt smashed the ball off the left post and Josée Bélanger one-timed the rebound towards goal. Verónica Pérez made a terrific leaping save that pushed Bélanger's shot over the crossbar, but it was completely illegal because she wasn't the goalkeeper. So Pérez was ejected and Sinclair scored on the ensuing penalty against Mexico's actual goalkeeper, Erika Vanegas.

Sinclair's 1-0 goal in the 2010 Concacaf Championship Final secured Canada their second confederation title and their first major trophy in 12 years. Sinclair scored the match winner in the 54th minute after which Canada held back the hosts Mexico for another 36-plus minutes in front of a pro-Mexican crowd of 16,005 spectators at the Estadio Quintana Roo in Cancún.

2010 Concacaf Women's World Cup Qualifying

Both Canada and Mexico had already qualified for the FIFA World Cup by the time they faced each other in the 2010 Concacaf Final. Canada qualified three days earlier with a 4-0 win over Costa Rica while Mexico qualified on the same night with a shock 2-1 win over USA who were the reigning Olympic champions. The United States then beat Costa Rica for third place and later beat Italy in a two-match intercontinental playoff series to qualify for the 2011 FIFA World Cup in Germany.

Across five matches at the Concacaf Championship, Canada outscored their opponents 17-0 and tied program records with six consecutive wins (starting with a friendly at Toronto) and five consecutive clean sheets. Sinclair led Canada with six goals, two less than tournament leader Abby Wambach who scored eight for the United States. While there were no official trophies awarded at the conclusion of the competition, Sinclair could have been named the Top Player while Karina LeBlanc could have been named the Top Goalkeeper.

With five matches in 11 days, Head Coach Carolina Morace rotated her squad across the tournament, but still featured Sinclair and centre back Candace Chapman in every minute of every match. Five players started every match while nine players started both the Semifinals and the Concacaf Final.

CANADIAN LEGEND • CANDACE CHAPMAN

Candace Chapman was the first Olympic medal winner inducted by the Canada Soccer Hall of Fame when she was honoured as part of the Class of 2018. The Canadian centre back won an Olympic Bronze Medal at London 2012 in her last international appearance.

She was a Concacaf champion in 2010 and Pan American Games Gold Medal winner in 2011. In all, she won five Concacaf medals, played in two FIFA World Cups and two Olympic Games. She made more than 100 international appearances across an 11-year international career.

From 2002 to 2012, Chapman and Sinclair were on the pitch together 81 times for Canada. Chapman scored all six of her international goals when they were both on the pitch at the same time. They were also club teammates at FC Gold Pride and the Western New York Flash where they won back-to-back WPS Championship titles in 2010 and 2011.

Stadium, referees and lineups

CANCÚN, QUINTANA ROO, MEXICO - Monday 8 November 2010 at Estadio Quintana Roo (16,005 spectators). **REFEREES** - Shane De Silva (TRI); Cindy Mohammed (TRI); Veronica Perez (USA); Kari Seitz (USA).
CANADA - 1 GK Karina LeBlanc; 7 Rhian Wilkinson, 13 Sophie Schmidt, 9 Candace Chapman, 20 Marie-Eve Nault, 4 Carmelina Moscato (3 Desiree Scott HT), 6 Kaylyn Kyle, 8 Diana Matheson, 11 Josée Bélanger (16 Jonelle Filigno 74'), 12 Christine Sinclair captain, 14 Melissa Tancredi (10 Christina Julien 83'). Coach: Carolina Morace. DId not feature: 22 GK Stephanie Labbé, 2 Emily Zurrer, 15 Kara Lang, 17 Chelsea Stewart. Did not dress: 5 Robyn Gayle, 19 Brooke McCalla. Alternates: GK Gurveen Clair, GK Erin McLeod, Kelly Parker, Brittany Timko.
MEXICO - 1 GK Erika Vanegas; 5 Maria Castillo (15 Luz Saucedo 61'), 4 Natalie Vinti (14 Alina Garciamendez 43'), 13 Natalia Garcia, 2 Kenti Robles, 8 Guadulupe Worbis, 9 Maribel Domínguez captain, 10 Dinora Garza (17 Tania Morales 80'), 11 Nayeli Rangel, 18 Verónica Pérez ejected 53', 19 Stephany Mayor. Coach: Leonardo Cuéllar. Did not feature: 12 GK Pamela Tajonar, 20 GK Cecilia Santiago; 3 Marlene Sandoval, 6 Mónica Vergara, 7 Evelyn López, 16 Liliana Mercado.

The Canada-Mexico football rivalry

It may not be as rooted as the USA rivalry, but the Canada-Mexico rivalry has had a special history of its own since the two nations met for the first time in 1994. From 1998 through 2020, they faced each other in two Concacaf Finals, four Concacaf qualification matches for either the FIFA World Cup or Olympic Games, and two Concacaf matches that decided a group winner to avoid the world's number-one ranked USA in a Concacaf qualification match.

While USA have dominated the Canada-USA series, Canada have dominated the Canada-Mexico series with an overall record of 22 wins and three draws in 27 international "A" matches. In Concacaf matches, Canada have won nine of out 10 matches including both the Concacaf Championship in 1998 and 2010.

At the 2000 Concacaf Women's Gold Cup, Canada beat Mexico in the opening match which ultimately decided which nation finished second in the group behind FIFA World Cup runners up China PR. While the result may not have grabbed headlines at the time, it did feature a brace by 17-year old Sinclair, in fact the first two competitive Concacaf goals of her international career. Sinclair scored the 1-1 and 3-2 goals in the Canada 4-3 win at Foxboro Stadium near Boston. Charmaine Hooper settled the match with the 4-3 winner in the 87th minute.

"(Sinclair) has that special quality that I cannot teach her," said Even Pellerud in *The Boston Globe*. "She has the right genes to do it. She is just there and knocks the ball in with head, chest, or foot, and even if she plays bad she can score goals."

The young Sinclair was far more humble when speaking about herself and her scoring prowess during her first international season.

"I just go out there and try my best every game," said Sinclair in *The Boston Globe*. "Lately I've been in the right position at the right time. I didn't even expect (to start). It's just been going super well for me."

CANADIAN LEGEND • KARA LANG

Kara Lang was a Concacaf champion in 2010, her last international season before she retired through repeat injuries to her knee. Still only 24 years old at the time, she scored 34 goals in 92 appearances from 2002 to 2010 with Canada.

An honoured member of the Canada Soccer Hall of Fame, she represented Canada at two FIFA World Cups and one Olympic Games. She won four Concacaf medals and left international football ranked fourth in career Canada goals. She was Canada's youngest debutant and youngest goalscorer at age 15 in 2002.

From 2002 to 2010, Lang and Sinclair were on the pitch together 78 times for Canada. When they were both on the pitch at the same time, Sinclair scored 49 goals and Lang scored 25 goals.

Two years later, Canada beat Mexico 2-0 in the Concacaf Semifinals to qualify for the 2003 FIFA World Cup (at the time still scheduled for China). Another two years after that, however, Mexico shocked Canada with a 2-1 win to qualify for the 2004 Olympic Games.

That one loss still stings, especially on the heels of Canada finishing in fourth place at the 2003 FIFA World Cup. Canada were clearly the favourites to beat Mexico, but Mexican star Maribel Domínguez had other ides and scored twice before the hour mark.

Canada did get it right four years later when they beat Mexico in Mexico to qualify for the Beijing 2008 Olympic Games. Melissa Tancredi was the hero on that night, a 1-0 win in front of 19,850 Mexican fans at the Estadio Olímpico Benito Juárez in Juárez. They got it right again four years after that with a 3-1 win in front of 22,954 Canadian fans at BC Place to qualify for the London 2012 Olympic Games.

Speedy Sinclair an explosive player for Canada

In 2010 ahead of the Concacaf Championship in Mexico, Sinclair was on a role after she won the WPS Championship with her club FC Gold Pride and then helped Canada beat China PR in a home send-off match at BMO Field in Toronto. In that home win on Thursday 30 September, Sinclair got an assist on Diana Matheson's 1-0 opener and then scored the last goal for the 3-1 victory.

"We have some very taltented soccer players and for me it's about getting in the right position and they will find me," said Sinclair after the win at Toronto.

"It's not so simple," countered Morace sitting next to her in the post-match press conference at BMO Field. "It's just a champion that can do this."

Sinclair, still just 27 years young, was entering her prime as a footballer for both club and country. When asked by reporters what she thought was the difference in her game, she quickly acknowledged the work of Morace and her staff.

"She has brought a completely different method of training and we work a lot on explosiveness and speed work," said Sinclair. "For me it has been a two-year journey on that and it has paid off."

Sinclair shushes the pro-Mexico crowd

Six days before the 2010 Concacaf Final, Canada and Mexico faced each other to determine a group winner and, more importantly, who wouldn't face the Americans in the Concacaf Semifinals with a spot in the FIFA World Cup on the line (USA had already won their group). Of the two Canada-Mexico meetings in that year's tournament, the 3-0 group win is most often cited as the most memorable encounter from Canada's 2010 international season.

After all, there was far more pressure heading into the Tuesday group finale with a FIFA World Cup berth just three days away. This was also the first Canada-Mexico meeting since the 2008 Concacaf Semifinals in Juárez, so Canada were expecting some hostilities from a pro-Mexican crowd at the Estadio Beto Ávila.

Oh yeah, they played in the rain, the fans at the baseball-turned-football stadium were jumping, and Sinclair shushed the crowd after Jonelle Filigno scored the 3-0 goal in the second half.

Mexico had no reply against the Canadians, but they took it out on the Americans just three days later. After Canada beat Costa Rica to qualify for the FIFA World Cup in the first Concacaf Semifinals match, Mexico won 2-1 over the Americans to book the other FIFA World Cup spot in the second Friday night match. Domínguez scored early, Carli Lloyd replied for the Americans, and then Pérez scored the winner just 75 seconds after the Lloyd equaliser.

As for Canada's FIFA World Cup qualification in the first Friday match, it took them more than an hour to score the match winner. After Sinclair pushed the play deep in the Costa Rica zone in the 62nd minute, she fed Filigno whose shot was stopped, but the rebound went to Josée Bélanger who tucked it in for the 1-0 lead.

After the opener, Filigno and Sinclair made it 3-0 by the 75th minute and then a Costa Rica own goal from a Rhian Wilkinson cross in the 93rd minute settled the score at 4-0.

"We were anxious, we continued to make mistakes, but in the second half after we scored the first goal, all was easy," said coach Morace. "I told the players at half time we were able to score five goals just in the second half. They scored four goals and we dominated the match."

No pressure for Canada in the Concacaf Final

With Canada's qualification to the 2011 FIFA World Cup out of the way, there was far less pressure in the Concacaf Final on Monday night at the Estadio Olímpico Andrés Quintana Roo. This time, Mexico held the Canadians off the scoresheet until the second half, even if they did get the help from the crossbar in the sixth minute on a header from Melissa Tancredi.

"It was a pro-Mexico stadium, but it's amazing to play in that environment," said Sinclair. "Whether the crowd is cheering for or against you, it's just nice to see that support for women's soccer."

Sinclair scored the match winner, the lone goal of the 2010 Concacaf Final, in the 54th minute on a penalty kick after the Pérez handball. Sinclair made no mistake with her penalty as she picked the bottom left corner out of the reach of goalkeeper Erika Vanegas.

Behind Sinclair as she prepared to take her penalty kick, Mexican captain Domínguez was pointing to which direction Sinclair was going to shoot. Vanegas dove in the right direction, but Sinclair's kick was too perfect for the goalkeeper's reach.

With Mexico down to 10 players, there was little to stop Canada in the last 36-plus minutes. Mexico were physical, but Canada's defence stood firm. Canada won 1-0 and lifted the Concacaf Championship trophy for the first time in 12 years.

"Coming into this match, there wasn't a lot of pressure on us having already qualified for the FIFA World Cup, but to win a trophy is always nice," said Sinclair. "Our defence played incredible. To play five games without conceding a goal, I think a lot of credit has to go to them."

Sinclair lifted Canada's big, golden trophy in a sky of confetti, handed the trophy first to coach Morace on her right, then shared the trophy with her teammates and the team staff on the stage to her left.

After the trophy presentation, both Canada and Mexico gathered for a group photo as the two nations had qualified for the FIFA World Cup. Canada then boarded the team bus with the Concacaf trophy, returned to the Hilton Cancún hotel and continued their celebration well into the early morning hours.

GREATEST OF ALL TIME

UM GOLAÇO DA CHRISTINE SINCLAIR

TORNEIO INTERNACIONAL
SÃO PAULO, BRAZIL
SUNDAY 19 DECEMBER 2010
ESTÁDIO DO PACAEMBU (17,264 SPECTATORS)

Um golaço da Christine Sinclair

She just hit the ball as hard as she could. What a strike, what a finish, what *um golaço do Canadá, um golaço da Christine Sinclair.* The ball flew off Sinclair's left foot and goalkeeper Andréia was helpless in her diving attempt. From one end of the box to the opposite post and back in, the Sinclair screamer in São Paulo gets replayed countless times anytime fans discuss the greatest goals from her international career.

The Sinclair golaço was the tournament winner against Brazil in Brazil, the 2-2 equaliser in the 83rd minute with Canada reduced to just 10 players. The draw gave Canada first place at the Torneio Internacional Cidade de São Paulo because, across the four matches including the Final, Canada had a better goals record than Brazil.

Torneio Internacional Cidade de São Paulo

Canada won the II Torneio Internacional six days before Christmas after they went four matches undefeated with two wins and two draws. It was Canada's third trophy of the year following the Cyprus Cup in March and the Concacaf Championship in November.

Sinclair scored twice against Netherlands in a 5-0 win, she scored the only goal against Mexico in a 1-0 win, and she scored the equaliser in the Final against Brazil. Goalkeeper Stephanie Labbé was one of

---

CANADIAN LEGEND • STEPHANIE LABBÉ

Stephanie Labbé was the youngest of Canada's three star goalkeepers in 2010-11, notably winning the 2010 Concacaf Championship and then being selected for her first of three FIFA World Cups in 2011. While she got her first call up in 2004 and made her international debut in 2008, she had her breakout performances at São Paulo in December 2010.

Labbé came back to São Paulo in 2016 where she won an Olympic Bronze Medal. Five years later, she was in goal when Canada won an Olympic Gold Medal at Tokyo. From her 2020-21 season, she was a runner up in voting for the world's The Best FIFA Women's Goalkeeper.

From 2008 to 2022, Labbé and Sinclair were on the pitch together 75 times for Canada. Sinclair notably served as team captain when Labbé made her last international appearance on 8 April 2022.

Canada's stars of the tournament with clean sheets against Netherlands and Brazil before the Final.

These were Canada's first four matches since the Concacaf Final in November. While Head Coach Carolina Morace invited a few new faces into the squad, she mostly stuck to an experienced lineup across the four matches. She did start three teenagers in the group stage draw against Brazil, but then she went back to nine of her 11 starters from the November Final in Mexico to the December Final in Brazil against Brazil.

It was a positive result for Morace and her Canada side who were now just about six months away from the opening match of the FIFA World Cup in Germany. At the time, Brazil were a formidable opponent having finished in second place at three successive global tournaments since 2004 (Olympic Games at Athens 2004, FIFA World Cup at China 2007, Olympic Games at Beijing 2008). Brazil notably featured the game's best player, their number 10 Marta who was already a four-time FIFA World Player of the Year (*she won the award for a fifth-straight year at the conclusion of the 2010 international season*).

Stadium, referees and lineups

SÃO PAULO, BRAZIL - Sunday 19 December 2010 at Estádio do Pacaembu (17,264 spectators). **REFEREES** - Wander Escardine (BRA), Maria Eliza Correia Barbosa (BRA), Renata Ruel Xavier de Brito (BRA).
CANADA - 22 GK Stephanie Labbé; 7 Rhian Wilkinson, 9 Candace Chapman (5 Robyn Gayle 74'), 2 Emily Zurrer, 20 Marie-Eve Nault Y2R ejected 71', 8 Diana Matheson, 6 Kaylyn Kyle, 4 Carmelina Moscato, 12 Christine Sinclair, 11 Josée Bélanger, 14 Melissa Tancredi (16 Chelsea Stewart 85'). Coach: Carolina Morace. Did not feature: 1 GK Karina LeBlanc, 18 GK Sabrina D'Angelo, 18 GK Erin McLeod; 3 Laura Chénard, 10 Christina Julien, 13 Amelia Pietrangelo, 15 Shannon Woeller, 17 Brittany Timko, 19 Brooke McCalla, 21 Diamond Simpson, 23 Marie-Laurence Ouellet.
BRAZIL - 1 GK Andréia; 3 Aline captain, 4 Renata Costa (2 Marina 30'), 20 Erika (19 Danielle HT), 6 Rosana, 17 Fabiana, 22 Thais Guedes (13 Andrei Rosa HT), 5 Ester, 16 Gabriela, 8 Formiga, 10 Marta. Did not feature: Kleiton Lima. Did not feature: 9 Grazielle, 21 Francielle.

Three tournament winners in three months

Along with her tournament winners at the WPS Championship in late September and the Concacaf Championship in early November, Sinclair scored three successive tournament winners in three months. She finished the calendar year with 12 goals and nine assists in 24 WPS matches for FC Gold Pride as well as 13 goals and seven assists in 16 international matches for Canada.

This was also the year in which Sinclair became Canada's all-time leader in international appearances as well as Canada's first centurion goalscorer. At the pro level in 2010, she was named to the WPS Best XI and led the league with nine assists.

After Sinclair and FC Gold Pride finished in last place in the inaugural 2009 WPS season, they turned things around to finish first overall during the 2010 regular season.

With Marta added to their lineup through a WPS Dispersal Draft (after the Los Angeles Sol had folded), FC Gold Pride featured a new offensive quartet of Marta (19 goals), Sinclair (10 goals), Kelley O'Hara (six goals) and Tiffeny Milbrett (six goals). The four stars scored 41 of the team's 47 goals.

WORLD LEGEND • MARTA

A six-time FIFA World Player of the Year, Marta is a FIFA World Cup runner up (2007), a two-time Olympic Silver Medal winner (2004, 2008), and two-time Pan American Games Gold Medal winner (2003, 2007) with Brazil. She is also a league winner with professional clubs in Brazil, Sweden and USA as well as a UEFA Women's Cup winner.

Since 2002, she has scored 115 international "A" goals in 175 career matches. She won both the FIFA Golden Ball (best player) and FIFA Golden Boot at the 2007 FIFA World Cup in China. She was the first player to score in five-consecutive FIFA World Cups and she holds the tournament record for most career FIFA World Cup goals.

Since 2003, she has scored 10 goals in 19 matches against Canada. Five of those goals were scored in one game at the 2007 Pan American Games, a 7-0 thrashing in the group phase at the Estádio do Maracanã.

In the 2010 WPS Championship against Karina LeBlanc's Philadelphia Independance, Sinclair and Marta led the way en route to a FC Gold Pride win at Pioneer Stadium in Hayward, California. Sinclair scored two, Marta scored one and earned MVP honours, while centre back Candace Chapman helped the winning team post a clean sheet.

Just four days after the win in California, Sinclair and Chapman helped Canada defeat China PR in a home international friendly match at BMO Field in Toronto. It was Canada's first win over China in seven years (with four draws and four losses in between the two wins). The win at Toronto was also the first of a program-record, eight-match win streak from 30 September to 12 December (through to a 1-0 win over Mexico on a Sinclair match winner at the Torneio Internacional).

Road to the FIFA World Cup Germany 2011

Canada had a short three-week break in between the Concacaf Championship in Cancún and the Torneio Internacional in São Paulo. The tournament in São Paulo featured group matches just three days apart followed by a championship match just four days later on Sunday 19 December.

Since the group finale against Brazil was Canada's third match in a week, coach Morace decided to rest much of her lineup. She also went back to Labbé for the second time in the tournament and got a Player of the Match performance from the 24-year old goalkeeper.

While there were less than 4,000 in attendance for the Wednesday night group finale, there were 17,264 energetic fans in attendance for the Sunday early evening final at the Estádio do Pacaembu. Labbé was back in goal for the second match in a row while Sinclair, Josée Bélanger, Melissa Tancredi, Kaylyn Kyle and Rhian Wilkinson all returned to the starting lineup after not featuring at all in the Wednesday group match against Brazil.

The Sunday atmosphere was fantastic in support of Brazil, the recent back-to-back Olympic Silver Medal winners and FIFA World Cup runners up. Both sides created chances in the first half, but nothing dangerous enough to break the deadlock until the 43rd minute when Bélanger opened the scoring.

That first goal was scored in a quick flash. The ball went from Marie-Eve Nault on the left to Carmelina Moscato in the midfield and then deep down to the touchline for Tancredi to keep the ball in play. Tancredi sent in her cross from the left and Bélanger headed it home for the 1-0 lead.

Early in the second half, Brazil's number 10 Marta equalised in a matter of just six touches in eight seconds after starting her run from the midfield. She rounded the Canadian defence into the box with her fourth touch and then fired the shot past goalkeeper Labbé with her sixth touch.

Marta continually showcased her magic in that second half. When she scored the 2-1 go-ahead goal in the 72nd minute from the penalty spot, the crowd was chanting deliriously "Marta! Marta! Marta!" Her left-footed penalty was nearly saved by Labbé, but it was perfectly placed in the lower left corner.

It was actually Marta who had initiated the attack that led to the penalty against Canada, in truth an incidental hand ball after Danielle's quick shot hit Nault's right hand in front of the goal. Before Danielle's shot, Marta had danced her way down the left side with half a dozen touches before she crossed the ball into the penalty area.

Because it was her second yellow card of the match, Nault was also ejected by referee Katiucia da Mota Lima. Canada played the last 20 minutes with only 10 players and the Brazilian crowd got louder in anticipation of a tournament win.

Sinclair scores her screamer in São Paulo

All that changed, however, in the 83rd minute when Sinclair scored her golaço. From start to finish, the sequence lasted 23 seconds from one end of the pitch to the other.

It all started when Bélanger outmuscled her opponent for the ball in Canada's own end. Robyn Gayle won the turnover and cleared it down the right side for Tancredi who managed to hold off her opponents and play it further up the field to Sinclair. The Canada captain headed the ball and ran it towards the corner while Tancredi hurried up the field to support the attack. Sinclair then played it to Tancredi at the edge of the box, but Formiga pushed the ball back away from Tancredi's feet.

Unfortunately for Brazil's Formiga, the ball rolled perfectly into the path of Sinclair who let the ball fly towards the back post and into the goal.

"I thought I would hit it as hard as I could and it went in," said Sinclair. "It just came back to me perfectly, (the ball was) set up nicely for a one-time shot."

In the last 10 minutes, every Canadian played defence as they worked hard to maintain the scoreline. When Canada did get the ball, they often ran it to the sides or into the corner to kill more time on the referee's watch.

Eventually Brazil had a last big chance on a free kick in added time, but Labbé came up bigger with a leg save that kept the score intact. With the 2-2 draw, Canada won the tournament on account of their better goals record across four December matches.

"We did our best to turn the scoreline around and we managed it up to a certain point," said Brazil Head Coach Kleiton Lima in the local Brazilian newspapers. "But on the other side (Canada) is a very good team technically and with more physical strength due to the longer rest period. The striker Sinclair had the ability to hit a very nice shot and they deserved the title."

Canada celebrated the victory with a cheer for Christmas, the players and staff received their medals from the tournament organisers, and then captain Sinclair lifted the trophy to the joy of her teammates.

"It was exciting to beat Brazil in their country with this wonderful crowd," said Sinclair. "It shows that our team is strong and capable of playing well at the World Cup in 2011."

GREATEST OF ALL TIME

THE FREE KICK AT THE FIFA WORLD CUP

FIFA WOMEN'S WORLD CUP GERMANY 2011
BERLIN, GERMANY
SUNDAY 26 JUNE 2011
OLYMPIASTADION BERLIN (73,680 SPECTATORS)

The free kick at the FIFA World Cup

In the opening match of the 2011 FIFA World Cup against Germany in Germany, a broken-nosed Christine Sinclair hit a perfect free kick that flew over the six-player wall and past the diving goalkeeper Nadine Angerer into the top of the net. The goal, scored in the 82nd minute, split Germany's lead in half and shocked the 73,680 spectators in attendance at the famous Olympiastadion in Berlin.

Canada chased for an equaliser in the next 10 minutes after the Sinclair goal, but ultimately lost the opening match 2-1 on Germany's first-half goals by Kerstin Garefrekes and Célia Okoyino da Mbabi. As it turned out, it was Canada's only goal at the 2011 FIFA World Cup: in the next nine days, they lost 4-0 to France and 1-0 to Nigeria.

FIFA Women's World Cup Germany 2011

Canada finished in last place in their Group of Death and last overall at the 2011 FIFA World Cup after three successive losses at Berlin, Bochum and Dresden. It was perhaps one of the most difficult groups in

---

WORLD LEGEND • BIRGIT PRINZ

An honoured member of the German Football Hall of Fame, striker Birgit Prinz was a two-time FIFA World Cup champion (2003, 2007), one-time FIFA World Cup runner up (1995), and three-time Olympic Bronze Medal winner (2000, 2004, 2008). At the club level, she was a nine-time German Bundesliga winner and 10-time German Cup (DFB-Pokal) winner.

From 1994 to 2011, Prinz scored 128 career international goals, which at the time ranked third in the world behind only Kristine Lilly (130 goals) and Mia Hamm (158 goals). She was a FIFA World Cup record holder for goals scored (since passed) and a three-time FIFA World Player of the Year award winner (2003 to 2005).

On 27 July 1994, Prinz actually scored in her international debut against Canada, an 89th-minute match winner at Montréal's Complexe sportif Claude-Robillard. Eleven years later on 21 April 2005, Prinz tied Heidi Mohr's German national goalscoring record with another match winner against Canada, this time her 83rd career goal in a friendly at Osnabrück. In all, Prinz scored five goals in 10 matches against Canada from 1994 to 2011. One of those five goals was scored in the 2003 FIFA World Cup opener at Crew Stadium in Columbus.

the history of the FIFA World Cup featuring the reigning FIFA World Cup and European champions Germany, the Concacaf champions Canada, and the African champions Nigeria. The only nation that wasn't a confederation champion was France, yet they had only lost one match in their last 24 international matches since August 2009.

Head Coach Carolina Morace started the same eight players across all three group matches, six of whom played every minute of every match. The team showed well against Germany, but they were soundly beaten by France in their second match. Things went from bad to worse after they lost to Nigeria in their third group match. Just two and a half weeks after Canada's FIFA World Cup was over, Morace and her staff resigned on Friday 22 July.

As for Germany, they didn't win a third FIFA World Cup in a row. After finishing first in their group with three-straight wins, Germany lost to the eventual FIFA World Cup champions Japan in the Quarterfinals. Karina Maruyama scored the 1-0 match winner in extra time. After Japan beat Sweden 3-1 in the Semifinals, they beat the Americans on kicks from the penalty mark in the FIFA World Cup Final on Sunday 17 July (a 2-2 draw after 120 minutes, then a 3-1 win on kicks).

Stadium, referees and lineups

BERLIN, GERMANY - Sunday 26 June 2011 at Olympiastadion Berlin (73,680 spectators).
REFEREES - Jacqui Melksham (AUS); Allyson Flynn (AUS); Sarah Ho (AUS); Etsuko Fukano (JPN).
CANADA - 18 GK Erin McLeod; 7 Rhian Wilkinson, 9 Candace Chapman, 2 Emily Zurrer, 20 Marie-Eve Nault (5 Robyn Gayle HT), 13 Sophie Schmidt, 6 Kaylyn Kyle (3 Kelly Parker HT), 8 Diana Matheson, 14 Melissa Tancredi (17 Brittany Timko 80'), 16 Jonelle Filigno, 12 Christine Sinclair captain. Coach: Carolina Morace. Did not feature: 1 GK Karina LeBlanc, 21 GK Stephanie Labbé; 4 Carmelina Moscato, 10 Christina Julien, 11 Desiree Scott, 15 Jodi-Ann Robinson, 19 Chelsea Stewart.
GERMANY - 1 GK Nadine Angerer; 10 Linda Bresonik, 3 Saskia Bartusiak, 5 Annike Krahn, 4 Babett Peter, 6 Simone Laudehr, 7 Melanie Behringer (19 Fatmire Bajramaj 71'), 13 Célia Okoyino da Mbabi (8 Inka Grings 65'), 14 Kim Kulig, 18 Kerstin Garefrekes, 9 Birgit Prinz captain (11 Alexandra Popp 56'). Coach: Silvia Neid. Did not feature: 12 GK Ursula Holl, 21 Almuth Schult; 2 Bianca Schmidt, 15 Verena Faißt, 16 Martina Müller, 17 Ariane Hingst, 20 Lena Goeßling.

FIFA World Cup opener at Berlin

Sinclair had played in front of big crowds before, but the opening match at the 2011 FIFA World Cup was by far the biggest crowd in front of which Sinclair and her teammates ever played.

"I'll never forget being able to be part of that opening game in the 2011 FIFA World Cup in Germany," said Sinclair four years later on FIFA TV ahead of the FIFA World Cup in Canada. "Standing in the tunnel before leading the team out, Germany and Canada were standing there and all of a sudden they lift the barricade up and you can just see the (70 plus thousand) people."

At the start of the FIFA World Cup year in China, Canada played in front of crowds hovering around 10,000 spectators. After that, Canada didn't see another crowd bigger than 350 people for their next 10 international matches across Europe in Cyprus, Italy, Switzerland and Hungary.

At Berlin in front of a packed stadium, Sinclair nearly scored the first goal of the tournament in the sixth minute after Jonelle Filigno caused a turnover. Melissa Tancredi played it to Diana Matheson who in turn played Sinclair into the box. Sinclair dragged the ball forward from her right foot to her left foot for a shot down the left side, but her shot went high of the target.

From there, it was all Germany as they took a 1-0 lead in the 10th minute on a leaping header by Garefrekes. Before the end of the first half, Germany made it 2-0 on a goal by Okoyino Da Mbabi.

Early in the second half, captain Sinclair suffered a broken nose on an infamous elbow from Babett Peter. She refused to leave match and continued to play through the pain, even after Canada's Italian doctors tried to work on her nose. Then in the 82nd minute after she was tripped just outside the penalty area, she scored on that famous free kick to cut the lead in half.

Unfortunately, the score remained unchanged after another 10 minutes and Canada lost their opening match at a FIFA Women's World Cup for the fifth time in a row.

"We are more confident today than we were yesterday," said Morace. "We played a good game. We are not so arrogant to come here and say we are the best team in the world; absolutely not. If Sinclair had scored on that first chance, we may have been talking about a different result."

The broken nose and the Zorro mask

It was in the 47th minute of the opening match that captain Sinclair suffered her broken nose when she was hit by Peter.

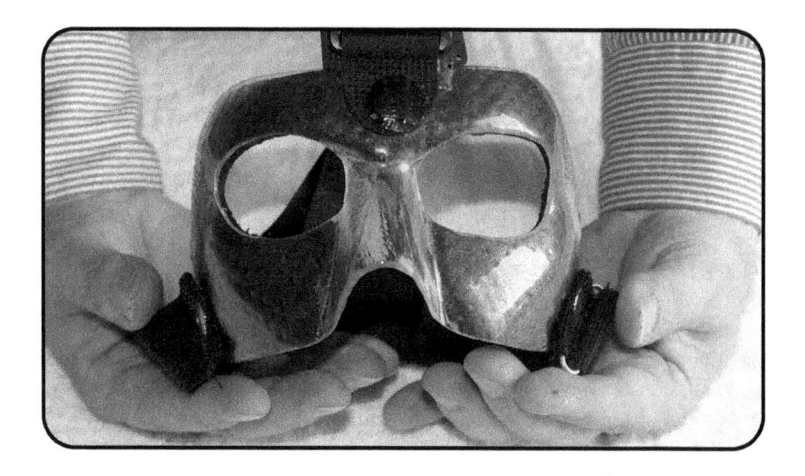

"The doctor came out, he's like, 'what happened?' and I told him I broke my nose," said Sinclair in the hotel lobby at Bochum when she met with reporters. "He looked at it and said, 'yeah, you did.' We walked off, it wasn't bleeding or anything and I wanted to go back on. They put some freezing stuff on it and he's like, 'you can't play.' That's when the whole thing happened. I'm saying 'I have to play, just let me back on the field. I'm fine.'

"He said 'you can't play with a broken nose' and I told him they do it all the time.

Neither Doctor Pietro Braina nor Doctor Salvatore Delogu were going to win this argument. Sinclair looked at her coach and she got the nod to go back on the field. From Peter's elbow to Sinclair's reentry, the whole episode lasted more than two minutes, with Sinclair actually off the pitch for just over a minute.

"Our coach sort of told me, 'if you can play, play,'" explained Sinclair a few months later in a Western New York Flash interview with teammate Ali Riley. "So I went back to playing and then after the game I went to the hospital where they shot my nose up and then they stuffed a metal bar in my nose and snapped it back into place."

Before Canada left Berlin, Sinclair was measured for a special protective mask that she would have to wear for the rest of the tournament. The mask was sent to Sinclair in Bochum and she wore it for the first time at training two days before Canada's second match of the tournament.

She called it her "Zorro Mask".

Sinclair played FIFA World Cup matches against France and Nigeria wearing the EproTec mask, but she didn't score and Canada lost both matches. Two weeks later after she left the FIFA World Cup and was cleared to play without the mask in her first club match back in the WPS, Sinclair scored two goals and got an assist as the Flash won 3-1 over Florida's magicJack at Sahlen's Stadium in Rochester.

A moment Sinclair will never forget

In the FIFA World Cup opener, Sinclair was pinpoint accurate with her perfect free kick against Germany. It was the first FIFA World Cup goal scored against Germany since USA 2003, thus ending a shutout streak of some 617 minutes.

"That is the danger of having a Christine Sinclair on the field," said former player Julie Foudy on American television. "What a beauty... you just can't hit it sweeter than that."

It was a skill that Sinclair practiced meticulously in training.

"I remember getting tripped up at the top of the box, (then) I remember just hitting it very cleanly, it got over the wall and their goalkeeper just couldn't quite get to it," remembered Sinclair. "It was pure joy. For a moment, we were able to silence the Berlin Olympic Stadium. It is just a moment I will never forget."

Sinclair's best free kicks for Canada

Sinclair has taken countless free kicks across her football career, but there are really just two worth writing about from her international career: the 2011 FIFA World Cup free kick against Germany and the London 2012 Olympic free kick against Great Britain.

Which one was better? Well, we'll let you decide because words can only do so much justice. *(Honestly, log on to Youtube, Facebook or Twitter and see if you can watch both goals for comparison.)*

The 2011 free kick against Germany was scored in front of more than 73,000 fans in the opening match of a FIFA World Cup. She scored the goal against Angerer, a future FIFA World Player of the Year, but Canada came out 2-1 losers after they failed to find an equaliser before the final whistle.

WORLD LEGEND • NADINE ANGERER

An honoured member of the German Football Hall of Fame, goalkeeper Nadine Angerer was a two-time FIFA World Cup champion (2003, 2007) and three-time Olympic Bronze Medal winner (2000, 2004, 2008). At the club level, she was a two-time German Bundesliga winner, three-time German Cup (DFB-Pokal) winner, and one-time UEFA Cup winner.

From 1996 to 2015, Angerer made 146 international appearances in goal for Germany and was named to the FIFA World Cup All-Star Team twice (2007 and 2015). In 2013, she was named the UEFA European Championship's Best Player, UEFA's Best Women's Player in Europe, and the FIFA World Player of the Year.

Against Canada, Angerer featured in goal seven times from 2001 to 2014 including the 2011 FIFA World Cup opener at Berlin. She posted clean sheets against Canada in 2001, 2010 and 2013. She wore the captain's armband when she faced Canada in 2013 at Paderborn and 2014 at Vancouver. She conceded goals to Christine Sinclair twice: once in a 2005 friendly at Hildesheim (Sinclair's milestone 50th goal) and then again on that 2011 free kick at Berlin in the FIFA World Cup.

The 2012 free kick against Great Britain in Great Britain was scored in front of 28,828 fans at Coventry (nearly 90% capacity). That goal was scored in the 26th minute of the Olympic Quarterfinals with Karen Bardsley in net, a 2-0 victory that pushed Canada into the Olympic Semifinals against USA.

On both goals, Sinclair took just two steps forward before delivering her right-footed kick on target. In both cases, Sophie Schmidt stood close to Sinclair as a decoy. While there were just six Germans in the wall in 2011, there was six Brits plus two Canadians (and then another Brit) in the wall in 2012. Her 2011 kick went over the wall into the top corner while her 2012 kick pretty much went through the wall in between Karen Carney and the 5'11" Jill Scott.

As for the two goal celebrations, we definitely rank the 2012 sliding celebration as her best, especially considering the two-goal lead in an Olympic knockout match. While her 2011 celebration was almost defiant, her 2012 celebration was simply full of joy: she ran past everyone on the pitch, back to her teammates on the touchline, her arms pumping and finally stretched out wide as she somehow slid beneath and into the most joyous group of Canadians in the stadium.

GREATEST OF ALL TIME

PAN AMERICAN GAMES GOLD MEDAL

PAN AMERICAN GAMES GUADALAJARA 2011
GUADALAJARA, JALISCO, MEXICO
THURSDAY 27 OCTOBER 2011
ESTADIO OMNILIFE (10,000 SPECTATORS)

Sinclair scores the late equaliser against Brazil

Canada left it late, but then Christine Sinclair came to the rescue when she headed home the 1-1 equaliser in the 87th minute of the 2011 Pan American Games Gold Medal Final against Brazil. The goal, scored at the near post on a corner kick from Diana Matheson, helped send the match into extra time after which Canada ultimately won 4-3 on kicks from the penalty mark. Up until that point in her career, the Guadalajara equaliser was the most dramatic late goal Sinclair had ever scored for Canada after the 85th minute.

Through four rounds on kicks from the penalty mark, Matheson, Sinclair, Melanie Booth and Sophie Schmidt all scored for Canada while Brazil's Grazielle was stopped by goalkeeper Karina LeBlanc. After Candace Chapman hit the post on Canada's fifth kick, LeBlanc stopped Débinha on Brazil's last kick so that Canada could celebrate their first Pan American Games Gold Medal.

Pan American Games Guadalajara 2011

Canada won the Pan American Games less than four months after finishing last at the 2011 FIFA World Cup and just eight weeks after newly-appointed Head Coach John Herdman took charge of the program.

Across three group matches at Guadalajara, Canada won 3-1 over Costa Rica, won 1-0 over Argentina, and drew 0-0 with Brazil, but they finished second in the group behind Brazil after a drawing of lots. After a late 2-1 win over Colombia in the Semifinals, they won the Gold Medal after they beat Brazil on kicks.

With five matches in 10 days, Herdman rotated parts of his lineup against different opponents, although he started the same group of 10 players in both the Semifinals and the Gold Medal Final.

Captain Sinclair, who played in all five matches, came off the bench in Canada's third group match in five days, thus making this the first major tournament since the 2000 Concacaf Gold Cup that she didn't start every match. From the FIFA World Cup to the Pan American Games in 2011, only centre back Candace Chapman started all eight matches in both competitions.

Stadium, referees and lineups

GUADALAJARA, JALISCO, MEXICO - Thursday 27 October 2011 at Estadio Omnilife (10,000 spectators). **REFEREES** - Dianne Ferreira-James (GUY); Lucila Venegas (MEX); Rita Munoz (MEX); Mayte Chavez (MEX)
CANADA - 1 GK Karina LeBlanc; 5 Robyn Gayle (7 Rhian Wilkinson 80'), 9 Candace Chapman, 15 Shannon Woeller, 14 Lauren Sesselmann (3 Melanie Booth 77'), 2 Kelly Parker, 6 Kaylyn Kyle (13 Sophie Schmidt 65'), 8 Diana Matheson, 11 Desiree Scott, 10 Christina Julien, 12 Christine Sinclair captain. Coach: John Herdman.. Did not feature: 18 GK Rachelle Beanlands; 4 Vanessa Legault-Cordisco, 16 Diamond Simpson. Absent: 17 Amelia Pietrangelo.
BRAZIL - 1 GK Bárbara; 2 Maurine, 13 Karen, 4 Tânia captain, 5 Daiane, 6 Rosana (16 Ketlen 82'), 7 Francielle, 8 Formiga, 11 Thaís Guedes (18 Grazielle 107'), 15 Andréia, 17 Débinha. Coach: Kleiton Lima. Did not feature: 12 GK Thaís Picarte; 3 Renata Costa, 9 Daniele, 10 Beatriz, 14 Renata Diniz.

Coach Herdman takes charge of Canada

On Thursday 1 September, Canada Soccer announced John Herdman as the new Head Coach of the Women's National Team. He took charge at the Westin Crown Center in Kansas City on Monday 12 September as the team prepared for their first two international matches since the FIFA World Cup. Their daunting opponents were the world runners up USA for a Saturday match at Kansas City and a following Thursday match at Portland.

Herdman was given less than a week to rebuild the team's confidence and set their sights on London 2012. Right from the start, he introduced a new high-performance environment and pushed the players for two good performances against the United States. Without Sinclair and Chapman, both given a break after the WPS Championship, Herdman's Canada earned a 1-1 draw at Kansas City, then lost 3-0 at Portland (but only after the Americans were held off the scoresheet for an hour).

"This is a wonderful opportunity to work in a fantastic country and with a team that has the genuine potential to be the best in the world," said Herdman before he met his players in camp. "The focus is multi-layered, with the Olympic Games sitting just around the corner, my job will be to help the team achieve their podium goals while keeping one eye on the long-term preparations for the FIFA Women's World Cup Canada 2015 and achieving sustained success beyond this event."

Two weeks after the USA series, Canada regrouped in Vancouver and then headed off to Mexico five days later for the Pan American Games at Guadalajara.

Canada against the South American giants

Brazil have quite the global reputation when it comes to football. On the women's side, they have yet to lift their first world title, but they have come close as runners up at the FIFA World Cup in 2007 and as back-to-back Olympic Silver Medal winners in 2004 and 2008. At the heart of those three tournaments was their number 10 Marta, who from 2006 to 2010 won five-consecutive FIFA World Player of the Year trophies. At the 2007 FIFA World Cup, she won both the Golden Ball (best player) and Golden Boot (top scorer) trophies.

In regional and confederation championships, Brazil have won two Pan American Games Gold Medals (2003 and 2007) and eight of the first nine Copa América tournaments (from 1991 through 2022). They were also runners up at a Concacaf Gold Cup in 2000 and the Copa América in 2006 (the only time they didn't win the South American women's championship).

Before Marta came along in 2002, Brazil had faced Canada just twice in friendly matches played in the United States: a 2-1 win at Rapid City, South Dakota in 1996 and a 4-2 win at Portland, Oregon in 1999. That second match was less than three weeks before the 1999 FIFA World Cup when Brazil finished in third place and Canada went winless to finish in 12th place out of 16 nations.

The next time the two sides met was July 2003 at Montréal and Ottawa just a couple of months before the next FIFA World Cup. This time, Canada came from behind to win both matches by the same 2-1 score. Canada had 12,245 fans at Stade Molson for the first match and 18,078 fans at Frank Clair Stadium for the second match. Sinclair missed both matches because she was recovering from mononucleosis, but 17-year old Marta came off the bench in both matches.

In 2007, Marta became the first player to put five goals past Canada when Brazil scored seven in the Pan American Games group finale at the Maracanã. It was Canada's worst loss since Norway scored nine goals against them in 2001. Fortunately for Canada, the 2007 defeat was an anomaly: a year later, the two sides drew 1-1 in a friendly at Toronto before the 2008 Olympic Games in China.

In the next decade, Canada faced Brazil more often than any other opponent and the two sides posted an even record of five wins, five draws, and five losses each. The edge, however, went to Canada who beat Brazil to win the 2011 Pan American Games at Guadalajara and the Rio 2016 Olympic Games Bronze Medal at São Paulo.

Sinclair comes to the rescue late for Canada

Brazil were less than five minutes away from winning the 2011 Pan American Games Gold Medal. Less than five minutes, that is, before Sinclair scored the equaliser on a wonderfully-orchestrated corner kick by Matheson.

"Matheson noticed her corners were being picked up by the goalkeeper and she told me that on the next corner we'd get her on the near post," said Sinclair. "We got (a corner) and she went for it. The Brazilians were a little bit slow to pick it up. She put in the perfect pass and (my header) went in."

Sinclair's equaliser was scored in the 87th minute, not the latest Sinclair had ever scored, but definitely one of her most dramatic goals.

As a rookie in 2000, Sinclair scored a 2-1 match winner in the 92nd minute in the Pacific Cup opener at Canberra, Australia. Then seven years later at the FIFA World Cup in China, she scored what should have been the 2-1 match winner in the 85th minute to secure Canada's place in the Quarterfinals, but Australia's Cheryl Salisbury scored seven minutes later to knock Canada out of the competition.

At the start of Canada's 2011 campaign, Sinclair scored both the 2-2 equaliser and 3-2 match winner in the last 15 minutes of the Yongchuan Cup opener against the hosts China PR. Melissa Tancredi got the assist on both Sinclair goals, the equaliser in the 80th minute and the match winner in the 94th minute.

After the Pan American Games, Sinclair continued her habit of scoring late goals for Canada. In November 2011, she scored a 2-1 match winner in the 91st minute for Canada's first-ever come-from-behind victory over Sweden. Six months later against China PR, she scored the 1-0 match winner in the 93rd minute when she directed a Matheson free kick past goalkeeper Wang Fei at Stade Moncton in May 2012.

Less than two months later at Savièse in Switzerland, Sinclair scored a would-be tournament winner at the 2012 Matchworld Women's Cup against Brazil. Sinclair scored the 1-1 goal in the 92nd minute, but then Brazil's Marta weaved her way back around the Canadian defence straight from the restart and fed Grazielle for the 2-1 match winner in the 93rd minute.

Finally the biggest of all late Sinclair match winners was scored in the opening match of the 2015 FIFA World Cup at Edmonton. Adriana Leon was fouled in the penalty area, Sinclair scored the 1-0 match winner in the 92nd minute against Wang Fei, and the record 53,058 Canadian fans erupted in the stadium.

Canada win the Pan American Games

After 30 scoreless minutes of extra time in the Pan American Games Gold Medal Final, Canada won 4-3 on kicks from the penalty mark to beat Brazil. Canadian goalkeeper Karina LeBlanc was the big hero as she stopped the third kicker Grazielle and the final kicker Débinha.

"The kicks were not stressful at all," said LeBlanc. "Right at that moment, I wanted to stay calm. The goalkeeper doesn't want to get lost in that moment. What we try to do is stay focused and try to read the kicker. I certainly loved the ending."

It marked the third consecutive time that Canada Soccer won a Pan American Games Medal since 2003, albeit it was the first time that they finished on top of the podium.

"I can get used to wearing Gold around the neck," said Sinclair after the win. "It's absolutely amazing to be part of this team. We came from behind against Brazil, one of the best teams in the world. Not very often do you get to stand on top of the podium, so it feels pretty amazing."

The Canada players proudly took note of their significant turnaround since losing all three matches at the FIFA World Cup in June and July.

"This story is perfect," said LeBlanc to *The Canadian Press*. "We were knocked down after the FIFA World Cup, we fell down, then John came in and he said, 'what do you guys want?' We said, 'we want a Gold Medal.'"

Canada won the Gold Medal and it served as the perfect motivation heading into their Olympic year. The away win at Guadalajara also served as a pretty neat "gift" from Christine to her mother Sandra Sinclair back home in Burnaby, who followed the historic match on her 61st birthday.

"Happy Birthday Mom!"

CANADIAN LEGEND • ROBYN GAYLE

Robyn Gayle was the Semifinals hero that sent Canada to the Gold Medal Final at the Pan American Games. The Canadian right back came on in the 58th minute and scored her first international goal with just a couple of minutes remaining in the match.

Gayle was a Concacaf champion in 2010 and an Olympic Bronze Medal winner in 2012. In all, she represented Canada at three FIFA World Cups, two Olympic Games, and won medals at four Concacaf tournaments. After her playing career, she was part of Canada's team staff that won an Olympic Bronze Medal in 2016 and an Olympic Gold Medal in 2021.

From 2006 to 2015, Gayle and Sinclair were on the pitch together 64 times for Canada. At the club level, they went head-to-head in the 2006 USL W-League Championship when Sinclair and the Whitecaps beat Gayle and Ottawa Fury FC.

CANADIAN LEGEND • KAYLYN KYLE

Kaylyn Kyle scored her first competitive goal against Colombia in the Semifinals of the 2011 Pan American Games, the 1-0 goal in a 2-1 win to reach the Gold Medal Final. It was also her third of six career international goals, four of which were assisted by captain Christine Sinclair.

Kyle was a Concacaf champion in 2010 and an Olympic Games Bronze Medal winner in 2012. She made 101 appearances across eight international seasons and also played at two FIFA World Cups.

From 2008 to 2015, Kyle and Sinclair were on the pitch together 93 times for Canada. They were also club teammates for part of the 2015 NWSL season at Portland Thorns FC.

CANADIAN LEGEND • KARINA LeBLANC

Karina LeBlanc was Canada's goalkeeping hero in the Pan American Games Gold Medal Final, making two saves to beat Brazil on kicks from the penalty mark.

An honoured member of the Canada Soccer Hall of Fame and two-time Concacaf champion, LeBlanc helped Canada win an Olympic Bronze Medal in 2012. She was the first Canadian selected to five FIFA World Cups from USA 1999 to Canada 2015.

From 2000 to 2015, LeBlanc and Sinclair were on the pitch together 90 times for Canada. They were also club teammates at Portland Thorns FC and won the inaugural NWSL Championship in 2013.

GREATEST OF ALL TIME

SINCLAIR SENDS CANADA TO LONDON 2012

CONCACAF WOMEN'S OLYMPIC QUALIFYING
VANCOUVER, BRITISH COLUMBIA, CANADA
FRIDAY 27 JANUARY 2012
BC PLACE (22,954 SPECATORS)

Sinclair sends Canada to London 2012

With family and friends on hand at BC Place, Christine Sinclair scored two goals to qualify Canada for the London 2012 Olympic Games. With an energetic crowd of 22,954 fans in attendance, Sinclair scored the first and last goals of a 3-1 win over Mexico in the Concacaf Semifinals. It marked the second time in a row that Canada qualified for the Olympic Games.

Sinclair had a foot on all three Canada goals, two in the first half and the clincher just about 15 minutes before the final whistle. She scored the first goal on a pass from Melissa Tancredi in the 15th minute, fed Kelly Parker who played it to goalscorer Tancredi for the 2-0 lead in the 23rd minute, and scored the last goal on another Tancredi pass in the 76th minute. Sinclair scored the first goal with her left foot from inside the 18-yard box and her second goal with her right foot on a chipped shot over the Mexican goalkeeper Cecilia Santiago from just outside the box.

2012 Concacaf Women's Olympic Qualifying

Canada qualified for the London 2012 Olympic Games and finished in second place at the eight-nation Concacaf Women's Olympic Qualifying tournament at Vancouver, less than a 30-minute drive from Sinclair's home in neighbouring Burnaby, British Columbia.

CANADIAN LEGEND • DESIREE SCOTT

Desiree Scott was still a forward when she made her international debut in 2010 with coach Carolina Morace, but she was transformed into a defensive midfield maestro after coach John Herdman took charge of the Canada squad. Scott had her first Player of the Match performance at the 2011 Pan American Games and earned multiple Player of the Match nods at the 2012 Concacaf Olympic Qualifiers.

Fast forward to 2021, Scott was one of three Canadians alongside Sinclair and Sophie Schmidt who won back-to-back Olympic Bronze Medals plus an Olympic Gold Medal at Tokyo.

Since 2010, Scott and Sinclair have been on the pitch together more than 160 times for Canada. At the club level, the two went head-to-head in the 2022 NWSL Championship when Sinclair and Portland Thorns FC beat Scott and the Kansas City Current.

Still less than five months since Head Coach John Herdman had taken charge of the women's program, Canada won group matches 6-0 over Haiti, 2-0 over Cuba, and 5-1 over Costa Rica. After they qualified with the 3-1 win over Mexico, they lost 4-0 to the Americans in the Concacaf Grand Final with a record crowd of 25,427 fans at BC Place.

Herdman only featured Sinclair and Shannon Woeller in all five starting lineups, but he did start eight of the same players in both the Semifinals and the Final just two days apart.

Stadium, referees and lineups

VANCOUVER, BC, CANADA - Friday 27 January 2012 at BC Place (22,954 specators).
REFEREES - Dianne Ferreira-James (GUY); Stacy Ann Greyson (JAM); Milagros Leonardo (DOM); Cardella Samuels (JAM).
CANADA - 1 GK Karina LeBlanc; 7 Rhian Wilkinson, 9 Candace Chapman, 2 Shannon Woeller, 16 Lauren Sesselmann (3 Melanie Booth 63'), 11 Desiree Scott, 15 Kelly Parker, 13 Sophie Schmidt (17 Brittany Timko 75'), 14 Melissa Tancredi, 10 Christina Julien (6 Kaylyn Kyle 56'), 12 Christine Sinclair captain. Coach: John Herdman. Did not feature: 18 GK Erin McLeod; 4 Carmelina Moscato, 5 Robyn Gayle, 8 Alyscha Mottershead, 19 Chelsea Stewart, 20 Chelsea Buckland.
MEXICO - 1 GK Cecilia Santiago; 6 Natalia Garcia, 4 Aliana Garciamendez, 8 Marilyn Díaz (19 Mónica Alvarado HT), 3 Rubí Sandoval, 7 Teresa Noyola (16 Anisa Guajardo HT), 10 Dinora Garza, 13 Jennifer Ruiz, 11 Mónica Ocampo (20 Chrystal Martínez 86'), 9 Maribel Domínguez, 17 Verónica Pérez. Head Coach: Leonardo Cuéllar. Did not feature: 12 GK Anjuli Ladrón; 2 Arianna Romero, 5 Bianca Sierra, 15 Luz Saucedo, 18 Christina Murillo. Absent: 14 Renae Cuéllar.

Crowds build across Canada for women's soccer

When Canada won the 1998 Concacaf Championship on home soil at Toronto, the Concacaf Final drew an energetic, capacity crowd of 4,971 Canadian fans to Centennial Stadium. This was still a year before the crazy record crowds at the 1999 FIFA World Cup in the United States, so the Canadian organisers were quite pleased with a sell-out crowd in the Etobicoke suburb on a Tuesday night. It was, after all, a record crowd for a Women's National Team soccer match in Canada.

After 1999, the definition of a good crowd was forever changed. While Canada's opening match at the 1995 FIFA World Cup was played in front of about 650 fans at Helsingborg, Sweden, their opening match at the 1999 FIFA World Cup was played in front of 23,298 fans at Spartan Stadium in San Jose. After there were 16,448 fans for their second match at Washington, there were an incredible 29,401 fans for their group finale at Giants Stadium in East Rutherford, New Jersey.

SINCLAIR SENDS CANADA TO LONDON

In June 2001, Canada Soccer set a new home attendance record for the Women's National Team when they sold out Varsity Stadium in downtown Toronto: there were 9,023 fans in the stands for Canada's 2-2 draw with the FIFA World Cup champion Americans (incidentally, it was also Sinclair's home debut as an international player).

Then 2002 happened and the crowds got crazy big for Canada's youth team at the FIFA U-19 Women's World Championship at Edmonton (again featuring the young Sinclair). All six Canada matches drew more than 15,000 fans per day, with the knockout matches even bigger from 23,595 fans for the Sunday Quarterfinals (Sinclair scored five goals), 37,194 fans for the Thursday Semifinals, and 47,184 fans for the Sunday Final against the Americans.

For the Women's National Team in 2003, they set a new home attendance record three times in the build up to the FIFA World Cup: 17,282 fans for a Thursday friendly in May at Ottawa; 18,078 fans for a Sunday friendly in July again at Ottawa; then 29,953 fans for a Saturday friendly at the end of August at Edmonton. In all, Canada played five home matches with 10,000 or more fans in attendance each time in the year following the FIFA U-19 World Championship.

After the 2003 FIFA World Cup, Canada Soccer lost their momentum at home. The 2004 Concacaf Under-19 Championship was played in front of smaller crowds at Montréal and Ottawa (where Canada lifted their first youth trophy in front of just 3,300 fans), then over the next two years their Women's National Team home attendance peaked at 8,812 for a home friendly match against the FIFA World Cup champions Germany at Commonwealth Stadium in Edmonton.

After the men's FIFA U-20 World Cup in 2007, Canada had bigger crowds of more than 10,000 for Women's National Team home matches in 2008 and 2009 at the new BMO Field in Toronto, a soccer-specific stadium built for the FIFA tournament. After a disappointing dip to just 5,427 fans on a Thursday night at BMO Field in 2010 (and no home matches organised by the team in 2011), Canada returned to Vancouver where they hosted their first major women's soccer tournament since 1998: the 2012 Concacaf Olympic Qualifiers at BC Place in Vancouver.

The rest, as they say, is history. From 2012 through to 2019 before the global pandemic, Canada averaged 23,919 fans per match across 28 home matches including the Concacaf Olympic Qualifiers in 2012 and the home FIFA World Cup in 2015. From 2012 to 2018, they had at least one match every year with 20,000 or more spectators (their 2019 home send-off match before the FIFA World Cup drew 19,610 fans).

Sinclair makes the difference

While Canada blasted their way through the first few matches at the 2012 Concacaf Olympic Qualifiers, media were quick to criticize organisers for Canada crowds that hovered just below or just over 10,000 spectators. The opener, a 6-0 win over Haiti, drew just 7,627 fans to BC Place on a Thursday night.

By the time Canada played in the Semifinals with an Olympic berth on the line, organisers drew an impressive 22,954 spectators into the lower bowl at BC Place, the second-highest attendance ever for a women's international match played in Canada (and the highest attendance ever for a women's international match in British Columbia).

Another two days later for Sunday's Concacaf Final, there were 25,427 fans packed into that lower bowl at BC Place.

"The atmosphere was electric and the match had everything," said Herdman after the Concacaf Semifinals. "It was back and forward. We thought we had put it to bed in the first half, but you know the Mexicans are going to keep fighting and they did. The team just dug in, Sincy got the goal, and we knew we were going to London after that."

Sinclair was Canada's Player of the Match while her brace gave her 129 career international goals, third most in the world and one more than the retired German striker Birgit Prinz.

"I want to congratulate Canada who played very well and won their ticket to the Olympic Games," said Mexico coach Leonardo Cuéllar. "They have a player like Sinclair who carries a lot of weight on the pitch and she certainly made the difference."

Sinclair's second goal got the record crowd out of their seats with less than 15 minutes to go towards an Olympic qualification. Tancredi sent Sinclair through a pair of defenders and the captain simply chipped Santiago who was well off her line at the top of the box. Sinclair's goal gave Canada a commanding 3-1 lead.

Sinclair celebrated the goal with her arms outstretched to the home crowd who were now all on their feet.

"To qualify for the Olympic Games and to do it in your own backyard is a moment I will never forget," said Sinclair.

GREATEST OF ALL TIME

SINCLAIR'S HAT TRICK AT OLD TRAFFORD

LONDON 2012 OLYMPIC GAMES
MANCHESTER, ENGLAND
MONDAY 6 AUGUST 2012
OLD TRAFFORD (26,630 SPECTATORS)

Sinclair scores hat trick at Old Trafford

Christine Sinclair scored a magnificent hat trick at Old Trafford in Manchester in surely the most memorable of Olympic Semifinals in football history. She gave Canada the lead three times against the number-one ranked Americans, but the result ultimately went the wrong way after a pair of disappointing decisions by a Norwegian referee.

The Sinclair hat trick was her first at a FIFA or Olympic Tournament and her first against the Americans, in fact only the second hat trick ever scored against USA. She scored the 1-0 goal from a Melissa Tancredi pass in the 22nd minute, the 2-1 goal on a header from a Tancredi cross in the 67th minute, and the 3-2 goal on a header from a Sophie Schmidt corner kick in the 73rd minute.

While Canada's Olympic Semifinals match featured a bubbling crowd of 26,630 spectators at Old Trafford in England, the broadcast back home drew an average audience of 3.8 million viewers on Bell Media's networks including TSN. According to the broadcaster, "nearly one third of the Canadian population saw some part of all of the soccer match."

London 2012 Olympic Games

Exhausted yet resilient just three days after their Manchester marathon against the Americans, Canada won the Olympic Bronze Medal after

---

CANADIAN LEGEND • DIANA MATHESON

Diana Matheson magically scored Canada's last-minute 1-0 match winner to capture the Olympic Bronze Medal at London 2012. She had played every minute at midfield across Canada's six matches and scored the winner against France in the 92nd minute at the City of Coventry Stadium.

Across her international career, Matheson won the Concacaf Championship in 2010 and back-to-back Olympic Bronze Medals at London 2012 and Rio 2016. She played in four FIFA World Cups and three Olympic Games and notably left international football ranked second for Canada in career appearances, starts and minutes played.

From 2003 to 2020, Matheson and Sinclair were on the pitch together 184 times for Canada. Matheson was notably on the pitch for 105 of Sinclair's goals for Canada.

Diana Matheson scored a heroic last-minute winner against France on Thursday 9 August 2012. It was Canada's first Olympic Medal in a Summer Games team sport since men's basketball won a Silver Medal in 1936. While Matheson scored the 1-0 match winner, goalkeeper and Player of the Match Erin McLeod posted the clean sheet with the help of her teammates, her post and the crossbar. While they had a few half chances throughout the match, it was really in the dying moments that Canada put France on their heels with a string of successive attacks.

While the Americans won their third-straight Olympic Gold Medal since 2004, the 2011 FIFA World Cup champions Japan reached the Olympic podium for the first time by capturing the Silver Medal. Canada finished the tournament with three wins, one draw and two losses while the captain Sinclair led the tournament with six goals. Sinclair was also Team Canada's Flag Bearer for the Olympic Closing Ceremonies.

Through injuries and a small squad of just 18 players, Head Coach John Herdman featured the same 11 starters across the last four matches of the tournament beginning with their come-from-behind 2-2 draw against Sweden at Newcastle. After an emphatic 2-0 win over the hosts Great Britain at Coventry in the Quarterfinals, they played the United States at Manchester and then beat France back at Coventry for the Bronze.

Stadium, referees and lineups

MANCHESTER, ENGLAND - Monday 6 August 2012 at Old Trafford (26,630 spectators).
REFEREES - Christiana Pedersen (NOR); Hege Steinlund (NOR); Lada Rojc (CRO); Hong Eun Ah (KOR).
CANADA - 18 GK Erin McLeod; 7 Rhian Wilkinson, 4 Carmelina Moscato, 10 Lauren Sesselmann, 20 Marie-Eve Nault (3 Chelsea Stewart 101'), 8 Diana Matheson, 11 Desiree Scott, 13 Sophie Schmidt, 14 Melissa Tancredi, 12 Christine Sinclair captain, 16 Jonelle Filigno (6 Kaylyn Kyle 67'). Coach: John Herdman. Did not feature: 1 GK Karina LeBlanc; 9 Candace Chapman, 15 Kelly Parker, 17 Brittany Timko, 19 Melanie Booth. Alternates: 2 Emily Zurrer Injured, 5 Robyn Gayle Injured, 21 Christina Julien.
USA - 1 GK Hope Solo; 6 Amy LePeilbet (11 Sydney Leroux 76'), 3 Christie Rampone captain, 16 Rachel Buehler (4 Becky Sauerbrunn 110'), 5 Kelley O'Hara, 15 Megan Rapinoe, 10 Carli Lloyd, 12 Lauren Cheney (9 Heather O'Reilly 101'), 17 Tobin Heath, 13 Alex Morgan, 14 Abby Wambach. Coach: Pia Sundhage. Did not feature: 18 GK Nicole Barnhart; 2 Heather Mitts, 7 Shannon Boxx, 8 Amy Rodriguez.

Record 23 goals in 22 international matches

Christine Sinclair set a Canada record with 23 international goals in 22 matches in 2012, seven more than her previous record she set in 2007. She scored more than half of Canada's 44 international goals and was directly involved in 65.9% of those goals through either a goal or an assist (23 goals and six assists).

She was the top scorer at both the 2012 Concacaf Olympic Qualifiers in January as well as the London 2012 Olympic Games in July and August. Her six goals at the Olympic Games set a tournament record, one more than the previous record set by Cristiane (2004, 2008) and Birgit Prinz (2004).

Sinclair actually tied and broke her national record at the Matchworld Women's Cup in Switzerland in July, an important preparation series for four nations heading to the Olympic Games. Sinclair scored her record-tying 16th goal in a 2-1 win over New Zealand, then broke the record three days later on 17 July at Savièse on a 92nd minute 1-1 equaliser against Brazil (Canada lost that match a minute later after Marta's wizardry set up Grazielle for the 2-1 match winner).

Canada captures the Olympic Bronze Medal

In an epic display of resilience, courage, and the football gods finally having our backs, Canada earned their first Olympic Medal in women's football at London 2012. It took up until the very last minute of the match, but Matheson found the opening and scored the most momentous goal in Canadian soccer history.

Against France, the world could see that Canada were holding on to a thread in the second half, but it was a thread reinforced by the 36 million Canadians back home wishing them a place on the podium. Gaëtane Thiney hit the post in the 62nd minute and Élodie Thomis hit the crossbar less than 100 seconds later. Then in the 70th minute, a Corine Petit shot after a Louisa Nécib corner kick was cleared off the line by Canada's defensive superstar Desiree Scott.

The resilient Canadians just would not break.

"They've come to see the flag rise," said Herdman after the Olympic Semifinals. "That's the job. They came here for that and the job is not finished. They'll be disappointed tonight because it won't be Gold or Silver, but we'll take a medal from this tournament."

In the 90th minute, Canada got a bit of wind in their sails and won a free kick from a Sinclair rush. They didn't score on the play, but there was hope in the air as Kaylyn Kyle deflected the kick just wide of the goal.

Now more than a minute into added time and just three French passes later, Lauren Sesselmann won an easy interception and moved the ball back up the left wing. It went to Schmidt, back to Sesselmann, to Sinclair, a little spin in the box and back to Schmidt. Marie-Laure Delie knocked it away, but Matheson won it back with her right foot and played it to Schmidt in the box.

Schmidt stuttered, turned for her right-footed shot and hit the defender Sonia Bompastor. The rebound bounced perfectly, oh so perfectly, to the feet of Matheson who then scored the iconic goal.

"Unbelievable, unbelievable," said Herdman after he composed himself to speak on live television. "It shows the fortitude and resilience of these girls, we were never going to give that game up."

"This team is the most resilient team I've ever been a part of and it showed," said goalkeeper McLeod who posted the clean sheet. "They were coming in waves and we stuck to our guns and we came out with the win."

"It feels amazing," said Matheson. "We felt as a group that we were going to earn this and we did in the last minute. I am really glad we're not playing another 30 minutes."

"We're absolutely exhausted and we just battled and battled and got a few lucky breaks and we got one chance in the end and we made it count," said Sinclair. "We just won an Olympic Medal and nothing else matters right now."

Sinclair best Athlete, Canada best Team in 2012

Christine Sinclair won a lot of trophies and awards at the end of the 2012 international season. She won her 10th Canada Soccer Player of the Year award, five Canadian Athlete of the Year awards including the Bobbie Rosenfeld Award and the Lou Marsh Memorial Trophy, and two Canadian Team of the Year awards.

In voting for the Canada Soccer Player of the Year award, no other player came close to Sinclair: she received an incredible 54.1 points or 97.4% from a perfect score.

"It's a huge honour, but I actually think above all other years, this should have actually just gone to our team," said Sinclair of yet another individual award. "What we accomplished this year was absolutely remarkable and what I did personally I couldn't have done without my teammates. We had an amazing run and I think the credit should just go to all of us."

Against all Canadian athletes in an Olympic year, Sinclair won the Rosenfeld from *The Canadian Press*, the Marsh from *The Toronto Star*, the *QMI Agency* Canadian Female Athlete of the Year (later known as Postmedia), the Air Canada Athlete of the Year, the CBC Athlete of the Year and the Sportsnet Athlete of the Year. She was also named *Yahoo!* Canada Buzziest Canadian of the Year.

The two major team awards that year were *The Canadian Press* Team of the Year and the *QMI Agency* Team of the Year.

Alongside her major awards, Sinclair also won Canada Soccer's Player of the Month honour three times (May, August, December) and Canada's Player of the Match honour five times (including the epic Olympic Semifinals match).

"Christine Sinclair is the best women's player in the world," said Matheson. "It is just a pleasure to play with her and her performance in the Olympic Games was above and beyond even what she does every day and she galvanized the country."

Years later, Canada Soccer's Women's National Team was honoured by the Canadian Olympic Hall of Fame at the annual induction event held at Toronto on 23 October 2019. Most of the players along with coach Herdman and staff member Maeve Glass took part in the celebration.

Voting for the FIFA Player of the Year

One award that Christine Sinclair didn't win in 2012 was the FIFA World Player of the Year award. Instead, that award went to American Gold Medal winner Abby Wambach. The fact that Sinclair didn't finish amongst the top-three finalists, however, was a puzzle that sports enthusiasts across Canada just couldn't figure out.

On 7 January 2013, that answer was revealed when FIFA published the full list of selections from 305 different voters (coaches, captains and media). Sinclair finished fifth overall in voting, although there was barely more than half a percent difference between third-place Alex Morgan, fourth-place Homare Sawa, and fifth-place Sinclair.

The final results from voting were:
20.67% Abby Wambach
13.50 Marta
10.87 Alex Morgan
10.85 Homare Sawa
10.33 Christine Sinclair
7.99 Carli Lloyd
7.70 Camille Abily
7.51 Aya Miyama
7.32 Miho Fukumoto
2.89 Megan Rapinoe

When you broke down the scores by region or by ranking, the vote revealed some incredible discrepancies. The most notable discrepancy was voting for Marta by the world's lower-ranked nations. While she was typically the most skilled player in the world (example, her performance against Canada just eight days before the Olympic Games), she was not the best player in the world in 2012 and she did not have the biggest impact on the world's biggest tournament of the year.

So why did coaches and captains from nations ranked 81st or higher predominantly vote for Marta?

One can only presume that those national programs weren't paying attention or didn't care enough to consider the candidates properly. The final score from those bottom-ranked nations placed Marta first (18.5%), Wambach second (17.9%), and 2011 FIFA World Player of the Year Sawa third (14.3%). Sinclair finished seventh (just less than 7%).

Nations ranked 25th to 80th in the world were hardly better. They voted Wambach first (17.7%), Marta second (13.6%) and Morgan third (12.4%). Sinclair ranked slightly higher at sixth (8.6%).

By comparison, the top-24 nations in the world clearly watched the Olympic Games and considered the impact USA, Japan and Canada had on world football that year. They voted Wambach first (30.5%), Sinclair second (19.7%) and Lloyd third (11.8%). Sawa ranked fifth (7.8%) while Marta ranked ninth (2.7%).

By region, European coaches, captains and media submitted the most compelling vote: Wambach was first (23.2%), Sinclair was second (12.7%) and France's Abily was third (12.2%). Concacaf nations, on the other hand, ranked Sinclair (17.1%) behind Marta (19%) and Wambach (27.8%). Strangely, Asia ranked Sinclair last (2.9%), well behind Sawa (24.4%) and Miyawa (14.8%).

In the four other regions, Sinclair ranked fifth in Oceania (10.3%, one place behind Marta), seventh in Africa (6.9%, well behind top-ranked Marta), and seventh in South America (6.7%, three places behind Marta).

In case you were wondering, some of the voters that ranked Sinclair first were Canada coach Herdman, *The Canadian Press* writer Neil Davidson, Mexico coach Leonardo Cuéllar, Mexico captain Maribel Domínguez, Sweden captain Nilla Fischer, England captain Casey Stoney, and Norway captain Ingvild Stensland.

Of the 43 persons that voted Sinclair second overall, only 12 of them voted her second behind Wambach (the other 31 voters indeed ranked Sinclair behind any one of the eight other candidates). American journalist the late Grant Wahl notably ranked Wambach first, Sinclair second and Lloyd third (she scored two goals in the Olympic Gold Medal Final). German captain Nadine Angerer, meanwhile, voted Wambach first, Sinclair second and Sawa third. As for other voters, England coach Hope Powell voted Lloyd, Sinclair and Morgan, Australia coach Tom Sermanni voted Morgan, Sinclair and Wambach, while Wales captain Jess Fishlock voted Abily, Sinclair and Morgan.

From the 39 persons that voted Sinclair third overall, 12 of them also voted for Wambach first. In that group, Sweden coach Thomas Dennerby voted Wambach, Marta and Sinclair, Finland coach Andrée Jeglertz voted Marta, Wambach and Sinclair, Wales coach Jarmo Maitikainen voted Fukumoto, Abily and Sinclair, and Guyana coach Mark Rodrigues voted Fukumoto, Wambach and Sinclair.

Brazil captain Marta voted Miyama first, Abily second, and Sinclair third.

Marta wasn't the only captain who didn't cast a vote for herself. Japan's Miyama voted for teammates Sawa, Fukomoto and American Lloyd while captain Sinclair voted for Miyama, Morgan and Marta.

Not counting Miyama and Sinclair, there were 199 other persons that did not rank Sinclair in their top-three votes. From that group, 53 of them ranked Wambach first including Japan coach Norio Sasaki (he voted Wambach, Miyama and Morgan), France coach Bruno Bini (Wambach, Morgan, Fukumoto), and Germany coach Silvia Neid (she voted Wambach, Lloyd, Miyama).

USA coach Jill Ellis voted for Wambach, Morgan and Rapinoe while American captain Christie Rampone voted for Morgan, Wambach and Rapinoe. As for a few other voters of note, Denmark coach Kenneth

Heiner-Møller picked Miyama, Lloyd and Wambach, Switzerland coach Martina Voss-Tecklenburg voted for Miyama, Rapinoe and Wambach, Australia captain Melissa Barbieri voted for Morgan, Rapinoe and Abily, while Costa Rica captain Shirley Cruz voted for Abily, Rapinoe and Lloyd.

Canada's Olympic Flag Bearer

Before she left London in August with her Olympic Bronze Medal, Sinclair was selected to carry Canada's flag at the Olympic Closing Ceremonies. It was a huge honour for the Canadian soccer captain who had previously carried Canada's flag at the Pan American Games Opening Ceremonies at Guadalajara in 2011.

"This is a huge honour and I wish I could have my teammates right here with me," said Sinclair. "We want the next generation of young girls to dream of being in the Olympics and getting a medal around their necks. If we can instill in them just the belief that this can happen, then we have done our jobs."

Sinclair and her teammates all missed the London 2012 Opening Ceremonies because they were already in competition just north of London at Coventry (players and staff watched the event as a group on television at the Chesford Grange Hotel near Warwick). For the Closing Ceremonies, the team was back at the Olympic Village, so all the players and staff were able to walk to the live event at London's Olympic Stadium.

Sinclair's selection was a popular decision with fans back home, some of whom started an online campaign shortly after her historic hat trick and before the soccer team had an even secured an Olympic Medal (Sinclair joked that it was probably her teammates behind the campaign).

When Team Canada's Chef de Mission Mark Tewksbury called to give her the good news before the official announcement, Sinclair missed the messages for several hours before she finally called back.

"I was away at track and field and our cell phones don't work in some of the venues, so (when) I got away, there were missed calls and texts that read 'Mark needs to get a hold of you now," explained Sinclair after she was introduced to the media the following day.

"He was like you can't tell anyone... but I called my mom."

The Theatre of Dreams

More than 10 years have passed since the Manchester match and Canadians have yet to experience another sporting event as exhilarating and upsetting as those Olympic Semifinals.

"It was the first time that a Canadian team went blow to blow with them and created just as many chances as they did," said Sinclair five years later in an interview for CanadaSoccerTV. "I remember going up 1-0, then 1-1, 2-1, 2-2, 3-2, 3-3... individually, it was just one of those games that you dream of that everything you seem to shoot goes in..."

"You can't find greatness until you have moments like that," said coach Herdman. "Christine had scored a lot of goals throughout her career, but that was her defining moment. What I loved about Christine in that game was that steely determination to do what she does well, which is 'every chance I get, I am taking it for you girls.' And these women said, 'alright we're not just defending this game, we're going to give you more chances Christine, but you better take them' and she did."

To this day, there is little to write about how the match ended, but if you're brave you can still go back and watch those first 75 minutes with Canada still leading 3-2.

"I've never been more proud of my teammates, I've never been more proud to represent Canada," said Sinclair. "The game at the (2002 FIFA) Under-19 Final sort of put soccer on the map in this country, but then that game (in 2012) just blew it wide open. Hopefully we inspired a nation, inspired a generation of young girls to dream of representing their country."

Some of those young players watching in 2012 have already made an impact. They helped Canada win an Olympic Bronze Medal at Rio 2016 and then an Olympic Gold Medal at Tokyo in 2021.

"Sincy was not a human being that game," said Tancredi. "She was like a little goalscoring robot. She had that cruise control, you could see it in her eyes. There wasn't that emotion, but you could see that stoic appearance... you can see when her jaw clenches a bit and she just knows and her eyes just pierce right through you, those blue eyes..."

"She did what Sincy has always done, but she just did it all in one game and blew the minds of everyone there, blew the minds of the 10.7 million Canadians that tuned in that day. She was automatic that game."

CANADIAN LEGEND • ERIN McLEOD

Erin McLeod was Canada's star goalkeeper at the London 2012 Olympic Games, notably posting the 1-0 clean sheet and earning Canada's Player of the Match honours in the Bronze Medal match against France.

Across her international career, she was selected to four FIFA World Cups and three Olympic Games, notably winning an Olympic Gold Medal in 2021 at Tokyo. She left international football in 2021 as Canada's all-time leader in appearances by a goalkeeper.

From 2002 to 2022, McLeod and Sinclair were on the pitch together 110 times for Canada. At the club level, they both helped Vancouver Whitecaps FC win the 2006 USL W-League Championship.

CANADIAN LEGEND • CARMELINA MOSCATO

Carmelina Moscato was a rock for Canada at the London 2012 Olympic Games as the squad beat France to capture the Bronze Medal. Moscato played every minute of every match at centre back and was Canada's Player of the Match in the 2-0 win over Great Britain in the Quarterfinals.

An honoured member of the Canada Soccer Hall of Fame, Moscato won the Concacaf Championship in 2010 and was selected to three FIFA World Cups including a fourth-place finish at USA 2003. In all, Moscato won four Concacaf medals including Gold in 2010.

From 2002 to 2015, Moscato and Sinclair were on the pitch together 82 times for Canada. At the club level, they went head-to-head in the 2006 USL W-League Championship when Sinclair and the Whitecaps beat Moscato and Ottawa Fury FC.

CANADIAN LEGEND • MELISSA TANCREDI

Melissa Tancredi scored two goals and got three assists in four matches at the 2012 Concacaf Olympic Qualifiers. She notably scored the match winner that qualified Canada for the Olympic Games, the second time she scored such a match winner after qualifying Canada for their first Olympic Games in 2008.

A Concacaf champion in 2010, Tancredi helped Canada win back-to-back Olympic Bronze Medals at London 2012 and Rio 2016. She also represented Canada at three FIFA World Cups from China 2007 to Canada 2015.

From 2004 to 2017, Tancredi and Sinclair were on the pitch together 108 times for Canada. When they were both on the pitch at the same time, Sinclair scored 53 goals and Tancredi scored 21 goals.

GREATEST OF ALL TIME

THE PENALTY WINNER AT THE FIFA WORLD CUP

FIFA WOMEN'S WORLD CUP CANADA 2015
EDMONTON, ALBERTA, CANADA
SATURDAY 6 JUNE 2015
COMMONWEALTH STADIUM (53,058 SPECTATORS)

A nation erupts as Sinclair scores match winner

With the weight of a nation on her shoulders, Christine Sinclair scored the 1-0 penalty winner in the 92nd minute of Canada's opening match at their home FIFA World Cup in 2015. Sinclair picked her corner, took her steps to the spot and fired it perfectly past Chinese goalkeeper Wang Fei to the bottom left side. Inside Commonwealth Stadium, the record crowd of 53,058 fans erupted, the largest in-stadia crowd that had ever attended a Canadian National Team event for any sport in Canada.

Sinclair's goal secured Canada's first-ever opening win at a FIFA World Cup. It was also Sinclair's first-ever match winner in added time of a major tournament. On the play in the penalty area, centre back Zhao Rong's extended arms illegally pushed Adriana Leon to the ground in interference of Leon controlling the incoming ball from Jonelle Filigno's header. Referee Kateryna Monzul made no hesitation in blowing her whistle for the penalty.

FIFA Women's World Cup Canada 2015

Canada won their group and played through two rounds in the knockout phase before they were eliminated by England in the FIFA World Cup Quarterfinals. Ranked sixth out of 24 nations, it was Canada's second-highest finish at a FIFA World Cup behind their fourth-place finish at USA 2003. After setting an attendance record in their opening match at Edmonton, they topped that record at Vancouver in both the Round of 16 (53,855 fans) and Quarterfinals (54,027).

CANADIAN LEGEND • KADEISHA BUCHANAN

Kadeisha Buchanan won the Hyundai Young Player Award at the 2015 FIFA World Cup in Canada. The 19-year old centre back played in every minute of every Canada match as the team reached the Quarterfinals.

Buchanan helped Canada win an Olympic Bronze Medal at Rio 2016 and then an Olympic Gold Medal five years later at Tokyo. She scored her first FIFA World Cup goal at France 2019 and she won her third Canada Soccer Player of the Year award in 2020.

Since 2013, Buchanan and Sinclair have been on the pitch together more than 110 times for Canada. When Buchanan won Player of the Year honours in 2015, she broke Sinclair's string of 11 straight awards since 2004.

The next biggest crowd was the FIFA World Cup Final on 5 July in Vancouver with 53,341 fans in attendance. Some of those fans had barely settled into their seats before Carli Lloyd scored a pair of goals inside the first five minutes. Lloyd completed her hat trick in the 16th minute and USA won the Final 5-2 over Japan. While Lloyd won the Golden Ball as the tournament's Best Player, Canadian centre back Kadeisha Buchanan won the Best Young Player Award.

In all, the FIFA Women's World Cup Canada 2015 set a tournament record by drawing 1,353,506 cumulative spectators across 52 matches, the largest FIFA event outside the men's FIFA World Cup.

After Canada's opening 1-0 win, they drew 0-0 with New Zealand at Edmonton and then 1-1 with the Netherlands at Montréal's Stade Olympique. Canada won their next match 1-0 over Switzerland, but lost 2-1 in the Quarterfinals to England. Across the tournament, Head Coach John Herdman started the same group of seven players including Sinclair across all five matches and he started the same 11 players in both knockout matches against Switzerland and England. Sinclair scored against both China PR and England at the home event.

Stadium, referees and lineups

EDMONTON, ALBERTA, CANADA - Saturday 6 June 2015 at Commonwealth Stadium (53,058 spectators). **REFEREES** - Kateryna Monzul (UKR); Stephanie Frappart (FRA); Kelly Simmons (ENG); Outi Saarinen (FIN) .
CANADA - 18 GK Erin McLeod; 9 Josée Bélanger, 3 Kadeisha Buchanan, 10 Lauren Sesselmann, 15 Allysha Chapman, 11 Desiree Scott (17 Jessie Fleming 71'), 22 Ashley Lawrence, 16 Jonelle Filigno (6 Kaylyn Kyle 61'), 14 Melissa Tancredi (19 Adriana Leon 77'), 13 Sophie Schmidt, 12 Christine Sinclair captain. Coach: John Herdman. Did not feature: 21 GK Stephanie Labbé, 23 GK Karina LeBlanc; 2 Emily Zurrer, 4 Carmelina Moscato, 5 Robyn Gayle, 7 Rhian Wilkinson, 8 Diana Matheson, 18 Selenia Iacchelli, 20 Marie-Eve Nault.
CHINA PR - 12 GK Wang Fei; 5 Wu Haiyan captain, 14 Zhao Rong, 6 Li Dongna, 2 Liu Shanshan, 23 Ren Guixin, 19 Tan Ruyin, 21 Wang Lisi (18 Han Pang 42'), 10 Li Ying (20 Zhang Rui 62'), 17 Gu Yasha (8 Ma Jun 87'), 9 Wang Shanshan. Coach: Hao Wei. Did not feature: 1 GK Zhang Yue, 22 GK Zhao Lina; 3 Pang Fengyue, 4 Li Jiayue, 7 Xu Yanlu, 11 Wang Shuang, 13 Tang Jiali, 15 Lei Jiahui, 16 Lou Jiahui.

Rivals from Sun Wen to Christine Sinclair

When Canada faced China PR at the start of the 2015 FIFA World Cup, it was their 26th international meeting since the International Women's Tournament in 1988. In their first 11 meetings up until 2001, Canada couldn't beat China, in fact drawing only once while losing 10 other times.

In that span, China PR finished fourth at the 1995 FIFA World Cup, second for a Silver Medal at the 1996 Olympic Games, and second again at the 1999 FIFA World Cup. In the 1999 Final at the Rose Bowl in Pasadena, they lost 5-4 on kicks to the host Americans after a 0-0 draw. Brandi Chastain scored on the famous winning kick.

So when Canada eliminated China PR in the Quarterfinals at the 2003 FIFA World Cup, it was a pretty big milestone for the women's program.

Before the FIFA World Cup in 2003, superstar Sun Wen was sometimes the reason that Canada just couldn't beat China. She scored a hat trick in a 4-0 win at Montréal in 1998, another two goals in a 4-0 win at the 2000 Algarve Cup in Portugal (Sinclair's debut match), then another goal in a 2-2 draw at the 2000 Pacific Cup in Australia.

Canada's first-ever draw against China in 2000 was a subtle warning that the tide would one day change in their favour. Canada's two goals were scored by the 16-year old rookie Sinclair in the first 20 minutes.

In the 2000s, China failed to match their 1990s magic on the world stage, but after 2003 it wasn't until 2010 that Canada got another win against their opponents (Canada earned four draws in the next eight matches from 2004 to 2010). Canada finally turned the corner when they beat China PR 3-1 in a September 2010 friendly at BMO Field in Toronto.

After that home win, Canada beat China every time between 2011 and 2016, including the 1-0 FIFA World Cup opener on the Sinclair penalty match winner. With their July 2016 victory at Paris before the Olympic Games, they have won seven-straight matches against China PR since the September 2010 home match.

Incidentally, Sinclair's match winner in the 92nd minute at the FIFA World Cup is only the third-latest match winner she has ever scored against China PR. In January 2011, she scored a 3-2 match winner in the 94th minute at Yongchuan; more than a year later in May 2012, she scored a 1-0 match winner in the 93rd minute at Moncton.

Penalty precision

From 2006 to 2020, Sinclair scored 14 penalty goals for Canada. Her FIFA World Cup match winner against China PR was easily the most important, but she also scored a 1-0 match winner in the 2010 Concacaf Final.

After the 2015 FIFA World Cup, the next biggest crowd in front of which Sinclair scored on a penalty was the Rio 2016 Olympic Games (30,295 fans for the group match against Zimbabwe). In that 2016 match, there was far less pressure on Sinclair as Canada already had a 1-0 lead and it was only the 19th minute.

Sinclair's first penalty goal for Canada was scored against France in France on Tuesday 29 August 2006. It was the 1-1 goal just before the hour mark against Céline Deville, with both sides scoring one more time in the last half hour for a 2-2 draw.

Before Sinclair, Charmaine Hooper was usually the designated penalty taker. Hooper scored 11 career penalty goals for Canada between 1994 and 2004. Whereas Sinclair scored her penalties with her right foot, Hooper scored her penalties with her left foot. At the FIFA World Cup in 2003, Hooper scored Canada's match winner in their 3-0 win over Argentina in front of 15,529 fans at Columbus.

Hooper and Sinclair are still the only two Canadians to have scored on a penalty at the FIFA World Cup. Janine Beckie had a chance to join that group in 2019, but her right-footed attempt was saved by Sweden's Hedvig Lindahl. Beckie was Canada's top international goalscorer in 2016 and 2017 and she had previously scored against Lindahl from the penalty mark, but on this day Beckie was simply stopped on an excellent goalkeeping save from Lindahl.

As for the pressure on that penalty, there were 38,078 spectators in the Parc des Princes stadium with Canada trailing 1-0 in the FIFA World Cup Round of 16. Canada were eliminated that night after they failed to find an equaliser in the last 20-plus minutes.

Beckie was handed the ball by Sinclair, a veteran move that could have provided Canada with an added layer of momentum had Lindahl not made such a good save. In that moment, Beckie had a chance to score her first FIFA World Cup goal, a milestone that would have provided plenty of confidence for the country's top goalscorer from recent years. Also while Sinclair had scored against Lindahl plenty of times in the past (they were born just a couple of months apart), Sinclair was actually stopped by Lindahl earlier that year in Portugal.

Starting in 2021, Jessie Fleming has stepped forward as Canada's designated penalty taker. Sinclair will often be the first to pick up the ball before she hands the ball to Fleming. At the Olympic Games in 2021, Fleming scored both the match winner against USA's Adrianna Franch in the Olympic Semifinals and the 1-1 equaliser against Sweden's

Lindahl in the Olympic Gold Medal Final. She also scored on kicks from the penalty mark in the Quarterfinals against Brazil's Bárbara and in the Gold Medal Final again against Lindahl.

Up until 2022, Fleming has scored three penalty goals (including a 2022 friendly match at Montréal) and has missed only once (she shot over the crossbar at the 2022 Concacaf W Championship). On kicks from the penalty mark, she has scored three times including the winning kick against Lindahl in that 2019 Algarve Cup match.

An amazing atmosphere for the home opener

Sinclair will vividly remember the sound of that FIFA World Cup crowd before she took her match-winning penalty at Edmonton.

"When I picked up the ball, all I could hear was the crowd, it was very loud, so I just had to pick a spot and once I decided where I was going to shoot, it was just sort of letting yourself be okay with the result that's going to happen," said Sinclair. "Luckily it went into the back of the net and I don't really remember what happened from there."

Sinclair ran back to her bench, arms stretched, fists sometimes pumping, and a finger pointed to her coach before the group embraced her with open arms at the touchline.

"We knew China was going to be tough, we knew what they were going to do to us, we knew it was going to be frustrating," said Herdman in the post-match press conference. "When the call came, I celebrated like we had just scored because I knew that there was only one woman who was going to step up in the 90th minute and write the script like she always does. And she did..."

Sinclair was tremendously precise with her penalty kick, in fact picking the same bottom left corner to which she had scored her title-winning goal against Mexico in the 2010 Concacaf Championship.

"It was an amazing atmosphere to go out and play this opening match of the FIFA World Cup in front of 50,000 fans," said Schmidt, Canada's Player of the Match who sat next to Herdman in the press conference. "The Chinese sat back and challenged us to come at them. Finally something went our way. Then Sincy, oh Captain my Captain, came through and I'm just glad she put that in.

"Sincy is a special lady," continued Schmidt. "I think she is one of the best strikers in the world, if not the best. She's our captain, we put our faith in her and there was no doubt in my mind that she was going to put that away and if not, we were there for the rebound."

From that opening win, Canada got on a roll and finished first in their FIFA World Cup group for the first time in program history.

"Coming out of it, we're happy," said Herdman. "Three points, Canada are on a roll, we gave the fans something to cheer about... like I said, cometh the hour, cometh the woman. Outstanding from Christine Sinclair. The sort of pressure on her, there's only one woman in the world that can get up and do that."

Record-breaking television numbers

For the win, Bell Media reported record-breaking numbers across their channels CTV, TSN and RDS: 1.8 million viewers watched the opener, the most ever for a FIFA Women's World Cup match on Canadian TV.

"Overall, 5.6 million unique Canadian viewers tuned in for some or all of the Canada-China PR match, which took place in front of a record crowd in Edmonton," wrote Bell Media. "Audience levels peaked at 2.6 million viewers as captain Christine Sinclair stepped up for Canada and calmly slotted home a penalty in added time."

By the time the FIFA World Cup wrapped up a month later, more than 20 million Canadians had watched at least part of the competition.

For Canada's Quarterfinals match, Bell Media said they reached 3.2 million Canadian viewers, the second-biggest television audience for the Women's National Team behind only the London 2012 Semifinals. Overall, Bell Media said the Quarterfinals reached 7.5 million unique Canadian viewers and the audience peaked at 4.3 million viewers.

"You have these ideas of what it is going to be like, but that first game against China, I've never experienced anything quite like that," said Sinclair back home in Portland. "Then to get the chance to play a couple of games in my hometown, it's something I'll never forget. It's a once-in-a-lifetime chance to get to play a home FIFA World Cup and have 50,000 fans cheering for you and rooting for your team. You know, we did alright and the crowd support was incredible. Those are definitely some of the highlights from the tournament."

GREATEST OF ALL TIME

WONDER GOAL SENDS CANADA TO RIO

CONCACAF WOMEN'S OLYMPIC QUALIFYING
HOUSTON, TEXAS, USA
FRIDAY 19 FEBRUARY 2016
BBVA COMPASS STADIUM (5,516 SPECTATORS)

Wonder goal sends Canada to Rio 2016

At the 2016 Concacaf Olympic Qualifiers, Christine Sinclair scored an all-world match winner that qualified Canada to the Olympic Games for the third time in a row. It was a highlight-reel goal shown around the world after she lifted the ball with her right foot and then spun and fired with her left foot a shot that went off the crossbar and into the goal to beat Costa Rica goalkeeper Dinnia Díaz.

It was Sinclair's second goal of the match, a Friday night 3-1 win at Houston that paved the way for Canada's return to the Olympic podium six months later. It was also the second-straight Olympic qualification match in which Sinclair scored two goals in a 3-1 win, a feat she performed four years earlier at Vancouver when Canada eliminated Mexico on the road to the London 2012 Olympic Games.

2016 Concacaf Women's Olympic Qualifying

Canada qualified for the Rio 2016 Olympic Games and finished second at the Concacaf Olympic Qualifying Tournament behind confederation champions USA. In the group phase, Canada won 5-0 over Guyana, 6-0 over Trinidad and Tobago, and 10-0 over Guatemala. In the knockout phase, they won 3-1 over Costa Rica to qualify for the Olympic Games, but then lost 2-0 to USA in the Concacaf Grand Final.

Centre backs Kadeisha Buchanan and Shelina Zadorsky were the only two players that started all five matches as Head Coach John Herdman rotated his squad to keep his players fresh across the tournament. In the knockout phase, only six players started both the matches against Costa Rica and USA. Sinclair herself was well rested for the Concacaf Semifinals: after she featured in the opener and scored as a substitute in the second match, she rested on the bench for the last group match before the Concacaf Semifinals.

Stadium, referees and lineups

HOUSTON, TEXAS, USA - Friday 19 February 2016 at BBVA Compass Stadium (5,516 spectators). REFEREES - Melissa Borjas (HON); Shirley Perello (HON); Stacy-Ann Greyson (JAM); Gillian Martindale (JAM)
CANADA - 18 GK Erin McLeod; 9 Josée Bélanger, 3 Kadeisha Buchanan, 4 Shelina Zadorsky, 2 Allysha Chapman, 11 Desiree Scott, 13 Sophie Schmidt (15 Nichelle Prince 83'), 10 Ashley Lawrence, 8 Diana Matheson, 6 Deanne Rose (6 Quinn 90'+1), 12 Christine Sinclair captain (14 Melissa Tancredi 83'). Coach: John Herdman. Did not

feature: 18 Stephanie Labbé, 20 Sabrina D'Angelo; 7 Rhian Wilkinson, 16 Gabrielle Carle, 17 Jessie Fleming, 19 Janine Beckie.
COSTA RICA - 1 GK Dinnia Díaz; 5 Diana Sáenz, 6 Carol Sánchez, 20 Wendy Acosta, 12 Lixy Rodríguez, 16 Katherine Alvarado (19 Fabiola Sánchez 90'), 15 Cristín Granados, 10 Shirley Cruz captain, 7 Mélissa Herrera, 14 Maria Barrantes (17 Karla Villalobos 61'), 11 Raquel Rodríguez. Head coach: Amelia Valverde. Did not feature: 13 GK Yalitza Sanchez, 18 GK Yuliana Salas; 2 Gabriela Guillén, 3 Gloriana Villalobos, 4 Mariana Benavides, 8 Daniela Cruz, 9 Carolina Venegas.

Sinclair passes legend Mia Hamm

Sinclair scored her milestone 159th international goal at the Concacaf Olympic Qualifiers to pass Mia Hamm for the second most international goals in football history. After Sinclair got a pair of assists in the opener (Ashley Lawrence recorded her first career hat trick in the 5-0 win over Guyana), Sinclair reached the milestone in the 63rd minute of a 6-0 win over Trinidad and Tobago.

"It is a huge honour, one of those things I didn't think I would reach when I started out," said Sinclair.

Hamm was the first big American goalscoring superstar of women's football in the 1990s. She made her international debut in 1987 at age 15 and simultaneously played for the American youth team as a teen. With the full National Team, she scored her first international goal on 25 July 1990 at Winnipeg against Norway, then scored her first goal against Canada two days later in a 4-1 win at the Winnipeg Soccer

WORLD LEGEND • MIA HAMM

An honoured member of the U.S. Soccer Hall of Fame, Mia Hamm is a two-time FIFA World Cup champion (1991, 1999), a two-time Olympic Gold Medal winner (1996, 2004), and one-time Olympic Silver Medal winner (2000). At the club level, she was a WUSA Founder's Cup winner with the Washington Freedom.

From 1987 to 2004, she scored a world-record 158 international "A" goals in 276 matches, a record only passed by Abby Wambach and then Christine Sinclair. She was also a five-time U.S. Soccer Athlete of the Year and two-time FIFA World Player of the Year.

With USA, Hamm scored 14 goals in 24 career matches against Canada, the second-most ever behind only Tiffeny Milbrett (18). She notably scored the match winners against Canada to capture the 1994 Concacaf Championship at Montréal and the 2002 Concacaf Gold Cup at Pasadena.

THE WONDER GOAL

Complex. Hamm's goal against Canada was scored after an interception late in the first half: she moved in on the right side and beat goalkeeper Carla Chin on the short side with a low, right-footed shot.

Just over a year later and still a teenager, Hamm was a FIFA World Cup champion in China after a 2-1 win over Norway in the Final. Hamm scored two goals in her first FIFA World Cup.

By the time Hamm suited up for USA's home FIFA World Cup in 1999, the 27-year old forward was also an Olympic champion with more than 100 international goals to her credit. That was the year Sinclair watched in awe as 16 National Teams played in front of record-breaking crowds across the United States. Sinclair even attended matches in Portland.

Hamm and the Americans won the 1999 FIFA World Cup on the last day after they beat China PR on kicks from the penalty mark. Inside the Rose Bowl, there were 90,185 fans in attendance for the historic FIFA World Cup Final at Pasadena in California.

When Hamm hung up her Hall of Fame boots in 2004, she had won two Olympic Gold Medals to go alongside her two FIFA World Cup titles. Her last goal against Canada was the golden goal winner in the 2002 Concacaf Gold Cup Final while her 158th and last international goal was scored two years later at Giants Stadium in a 2004 friendly against Denmark.

So when Sinclair passed former world record holder Hamm on the world's all-time international goalscoring list, it was a special moment for Sinclair who as a teenager idolized Hamm.

"As a kid growing up, Mia Hamm was the face of soccer," said Sinclair. "I remember thinking after my first year or two on the National Team, 'she had so many goals, how is anyone ever going to reach that level?' So to pass her this year, for me it was one of those moments that was pretty cool and something that I will never forget."

Her teammates were equally impressed, but in truth just as much with their captain Christine Sinclair as the legend Mia Hamm.

"It's kind of surreal to be able to say that I played with (Sinclair) all these years," said Diana Matheson. "We (the older players) grew up watching Mia Hamm. The young kids not so much (and) they know less and less who Mia Hamm is, but Mia Hamm was just so big and such an amazing player and now Christine has passed her. I have no doubt that (Christine) is going to pass Abby (Wambach) eventually, too.

"For a country like Canada who doesn't play as many matches, doesn't beat teams eight- or 10-nothing, for (Christine) to score that many goals over the years is just an incredible accomplishment. It's pretty unbelievable what she has done."

Canada qualify for the Rio 2016 Olympic Games

From the Olympic Games at London 2012 to the home FIFA World Cup in 2015, coach Herdman kept 15 Bronze Medal winners and added eight new players. In less than a year from the FIFA World Cup in 2015 to the Concacaf Olympic Qualifiers in 2016, Herdman kept just 13 players from 2015 and introduced seven new players.

At the end of the day, it was the 17-year international veteran Christine Sinclair who led Canada to their Olympic qualification with a pair of goals against Costa Rica.

"She brings a confidence to this team that I have always imagined you have to have in a captain," said 16-year old Deanne Rose who was barely a year old when Sinclair made her international debut in March 2000. "It was just great to see her go and score those two goals and secure our win."

After just 17 minutes in the Concacaf Semifinals, Sinclair put Canada in the lead on a right-footed volley from inside the box. On the play, Josée Bélanger floated her cross over Rose and a pair of Costa Rica defenders before Sinclair controlled the ball with her chest and fired it past Díaz.

Early in the second half, Sinclair scored her wonder goal for the 2-0 lead in the 52nd minute. From start to finish, it was one of the nicest goals in history of Canada Soccer's Women's National Team.

"It was a whole team performance," said Sinclair. "Costa Rica is much improved and they tested us like no other team (at this tournament). We had lots of crosses into the box and I was lucky to get a couple in."

The wonder goal started with an Allysha Chapman interception on the left side. The ball then went across the backline from Chapman to Shelina Zadorsky to Kadeisha Buchanan and then to right back Bélanger. On the right side, Bélanger played it back and forth with Diana Matheson who then beat a defender and crossed it into the box. Cristín Granados knocked it away from Ashley Lawrence's feet and

Wendy Acosta had a chance to clear it, but instead everything went wrong as her clearance bounced off Lawrence and into the air.

Diana Sáenz had the next chance to clear the ball, but she botched her attempt and Sinclair ran six yards forward to shield the ball and show off her ball control skills with her back to Sáenz, Carol Sánchez, and Díaz. Sinclair was clinical with her shot and Díaz was cleanly beat.

"I hope that the team can count on me in big games because it is something I pride myself in being ready for these games," said Sinclair. "I think John (Herdman) did a great job throughout the course of the tournament resting players, so I thought we were the fresher team and it paid off tonight."

After the Sinclair brace, there was no turning back, not even after Raquel Rodríguez cut the lead in half from the penalty spot after referee Melissa Borjas called Desiree Scott for a foul on Sáenz in the penalty area. Canada eventually restored their two-goal cushion in the 86th minute after Rose scored on a cross from substitute and birthday girl Nichelle Prince.

"It's so awesome to always play for Canada and people like Christine Sinclair who has, like, two houses full of trophies and yet she's humble and never stops leading us," said veteran goalkeeper McLeod.

Coach Herdman was emphatic in his praise for the captain.

"She is class," said coach John Herdman after the match. "To all those people who had written her off at the World Cup, you know Sinclair, when you ask her deliver, she delivers. She has a lot going on in her life and she was injured tonight playing, but wow, what a performance. So stick with her Canada, we're going to Rio and we'll have another crack at that podium."

Canada's qualification at Houston meant that they had a chance to return to the Olympic podium after London 2012.

"We are pushing them to new levels, I think they are getting better and we will see where they land in Rio," said Herdman after the match. "They have firmly set a target of trying to be the first team to go back-to-back podiums for our country and that's what we want to do."

CANADIAN LEGEND • ALLYSHA CHAPMAN

Allysha Chapman made her international debut in October 2014 and featured in every Canada minute at the 2015 FIFA World Cup just eight months later. A Concacaf youth champion in 2008, she came into the full National Team six years later after her debut season in Sweden's top flight with Eskilstuna United in the Damallsvenskan.

Chapman then helped Canada win an Olympic Bronze Medal at Rio 2016 and an Olympic Gold Medal at Tokyo in 2021. She featured in her second FIFA World Cup in 2019 and won her fourth Concacaf Silver Medal in 2022.

Since 2014, Chapman and Sinclair have been on the pitch together more than 80 times for Canada.

CANADIAN LEGEND • SOPHIE SCHMIDT

Sophie Schmidt was an integral part of Canada's success in the Olympic Games at Rio 2016. She was notably Canada's Player of the Match in both the win over Zimbabwe as well as the Semifinals loss to Germany. She also scored an impressive match winner against France in the Olympic Quarterfinals, one of those goals she said "you dream about at night."

From 2012 to 2021, Schmidt was one of three Canadians alongside Sinclair and Desiree Scott who won back-to-back Olympic Bronze Medals followed by an Olympic Gold Medal in 2021. A Concacaf champion in 2010, she represented Canada at four FIFA World Cups from 2007 to 2019. She was Canada's top international goalscorer in 2014.

Since 2005, Schmidt and Sinclair have been on the pitch together more than 180 times for Canada. At the club level, they both helped Vancouver Whitecaps FC win the 2006 USL W-League Championship.

CANADIAN LEGEND • RHIAN WILKINSON

An honoured member of the Canada Soccer Hall of Fame, Wilkinson helped Canada win back-to-back Olympic Bronze Medals at London 2012 and Rio 2016. She also represented Canada at four FIFA World Cups as a player and one as an Assistant Coach. She won six Concacaf medals including the Concacaf Championship in 2010.

When Wilkinson left international football in 2017, she ranked third all time in Canada appearances behind only Sinclair and Diana Matheson.

From 2003 to 2017, Wilkinson and Sinclair were on the pitch together 165 times for Canada. Wilkinson was notably on the pitch for 87 of Sinclair's goals for Canada.

GREATEST OF ALL TIME

BACK-TO-BACK OLYMPIC BRONZE MEDALS

RIO 2016 OLYMPIC GAMES
SÃO PAULO, BRAZIL
FRIDAY 19 AUGUST 2016
ARENA CORINTHIANS (39,718 SPECTATORS)

Sinclair scores Bronze Medal match winner

Christine Sinclair scored the Rio 2016 Olympic Bronze Medal match winner against Brazil in Brazil to return Canada back to the podium for the second Olympic Games in a row. Sinclair scored Canada's second goal in a 2-1 win at São Paulo to upset the 39,718 Brazilian fans inside the Corinthians Arena.

With the win, Canada Soccer's Women's National Team became the first Canadian team to win back-to-back medals at the Summer Olympic Games since men's lacrosse in 1904 and 1908. The goal was Sinclair's third of the tournament and the 11th of her Olympic career.

Rio 2016 Olympic Football Tournament

Canada won five of their six matches at the Rio 2016 Olympic Games, notably beating the Asian champions Australia, the European champions Germany and the South American champions Brazil. After Canada beat Australia, Zimbabwe and Germany in the group phase, they eliminated France in the Quarterfinals, but lost to Germany in the Semifinals. Three days after the Semifinals at Belo Horizonte, they beat Brazil for the Bronze Medal at São Paulo.

While Canada led the tournament with five wins, Germany won the Gold Medal after a 2-1 victory over Sweden at the Maracanã in Rio de Janeiro.

CANADIAN LEGEND • ASHLEY LAWRENCE

At the Rio 2016 Olympic Games, Ashley Lawrence earned Canada's Player of the Match honours in both the opener against Australia and the Bronze Medal match against Brazil. She also set up Deanne Rose for the opening goal in the Bronze Medal Match.

Lawrence has already represented Canada at two FIFA World Cups and she won an Olympic Gold Medal at Tokyo in 2021. She won her fourth Concacaf Silver Medal a year later in 2022. She scored her first FIFA World Cup goal in front of 45,420 fans at Stade Olympique against Netherlands in 2015.

Since 2013, Lawrence and Sinclair have been on the pitch together more than 100 times for Canada. They were Canada Soccer's Player of the Year award winners in back-to-back years after Sinclair won her 14th award in 2018 and Lawrence won her first award in 2019.

While there were 52,432 in attendance for the Gold Medal Final, there was an even bigger crowd of 70,454 in attendance for Brazil's Semifinals match three days earlier (Sweden won 4-3 on kicks to eliminate Brazil).

Canada's Olympic squad featured just six returning players from the London 2012 Olympic Games, another six players from the FIFA World Cup in 2015, and six new players making a major world tournament debut.

Head Coach John Herdman rotated his squad across the tournament, with only teenager Jessie Fleming a starter in all six matches. In the back half of the tournament, Herdman started the same group of seven players including Sinclair across all three knockout matches against France, Germany and Brazil.

Stadium, referees and lineups

SÃO PAULO, BRAZIL - Friday 19 August 2016 at Corinthians Arena (39,718 spectators).
REFEREES - Teodora Albon (ROU); Petruta Iugulescu (ROU); Maria Sukenikova (SVK); Esther Staubli (SUI).
CANADA - 1 GK Stephanie Labbé; 9 Josée Bélanger, 3 Kadeisha Buchanan, 4 Shelina Zadorsky, 10 Ashley Lawrence, 11 Desiree Scott, 17 Jessie Fleming, 8 Diana Matheson (13 Sophie Schmidt 66'), 6 Deanne Rose (2 Allysha Chapman 59'), 14 Melissa Tancredi (16 Janine Beckie 69'), 12 Christine Sinclair captain. Head Coach: John Herdman. Did not feature: 18 GK Sabrina D'Angelo; 5 Quinn, 7 Rhian Wilkinson, 15 Nichelle Prince.
BRAZIL - 1 GK Bárbara; 2 Fabiana, 3 Mônica, 4 Rafaelle, 6 Tamires (13 Érika 63'), 5 Thaísa, 8 Formiga, 9 Andressa Alves (9 Poliana 57'), 11 Cristiane (7 Débinha HT), 16 Bia Zanerato, 10 Marta captain. Coach: Vadão. Did not feature: 18 GK Aline; 14 Bruna, 15 Fernandes, 17 Andressinha.

Canada's young players come of age

In the year after Canada's home FIFA World Cup, coach Herdman successfully integrated more young players into the Women's National Team ahead of the Rio 2016 Olympic Games.

"This is a really exciting time for us," said Herdman in February ahead of the Concacaf Olympic Qualifiers. "We have a leader in Christine Sinclair who really inspires the younger players, we have a group of experienced international stars, and a crop of young, hungry players."

Alongside future Players of the Year Fleming, Kadeisha Buchanan and Ashley Lawrence from the FIFA World Cup in 2015, Herdman added Sabrina D'Angelo, Janine Beckie, Nichelle Prince, Quinn and Shelina Zadorsky for the Olympic Games in 2016.

"These young kids have reignited the fire in all of us," said Sinclair at the Concacaf Olympic Qualifiers. "Training is very competitive, I think we have probably the deepest squad we have ever had, so it's exciting. I think the potential for some of these kids is just over the moon. We've got some special talent."

One attacking player of note was Beckie, who since the FIFA World Cup had been Canada's top goalscorer with eight goals in 18 matches (one more goal than veteran Sinclair).

In the month after the FIFA World Cup, Beckie scored two goals in five matches with Canada's U-23 squad at the Pan American Games. She then scored another two goals in four matches with the Women's National Team at Brazil's Torneio Internacional in December.

In 2016 starting with the Concacaf Olympic Qualifiers, Beckie scored six goals in 14 matches, making her the first player since 2003 other than Christine Sinclair to lead Canada in goalscoring ahead of a FIFA World Cup or Olympic Games.

From 2000 to 2015, Sinclair led Canada in goalscoring 14 out of 16 years, including 2003 when she finished as Canada's joint top goalscorer alongside Kara Lang (heading into the 2003 FIFA World Cup, Lang was in fact Canada's top goalscorer). Aside from Sinclair, only Aysha Jamani in 2004 and Sophie Schmidt in 2014 had otherwise led Canada in goalscoring during Sinclair's first 16 seasons.

In 2015, Sinclair scored more than 41% of Canada's 24 goals across 18 international matches (her ninth season with 10 or more international goals). By comparison ahead of the 2016 Olympic Games, Sinclair and Beckie combined to score just 31% of Canada's 32 goals (Beckie six, Sinclair four).

An Olympic record after 20 seconds

It took Beckie just 20 seconds to set an Olympic record and give Canada a 1-0 lead in Canada's opening match at the Rio 2016 Olympic Games. Beckie's goal was the fastest goal from the start of an Olympic match, about 10 seconds faster than Oribe Peralta's record at the London 2012 Olympic Games.

Australia had the ball for barely a dozen seconds before captain Sinclair stole the ball from Alanna Kennedy's feet, strode down the right into the

> **CANADIAN LEGEND • JANINE BECKIE**
>
> Janine Beckie was Canada's top international goalscorer in 2016 and 2017 as well as Canada's joint top scorer at the Olympic Games in both 2016 and 2021. In the Rio 2016 opener against Australia, she scored the fastest goal in Olympic history at just 20 seconds after the opening whistle.
>
> Beckie helped Canada win an Olympic Bronze Medal at Rio 2016 and then an Olympic Gold Medal five years later at Tokyo. After scoring three goals in the group phase at Rio 2016, she scored two goals in a win over Chile in the group phase at Tokyo in 2021.
>
> Since 2014, Beckie and Sinclair have been on the pitch together more than 80 times for Canada. From the first 79 matches in which they were both on the pitch at the same time, Beckie scored 28 goals and Sinclair scored 19 goals. At the club level, the duo helped Portland Thorns FC win the 2022 NWSL Championship.

box and centered a glorious pass to the feet of an unmarked Beckie. The young Canadian made no mistake in putting the ball past goalkeeper Lydia Williams from inside the six-yard box at São Paulo.

As it turned out, Beckie's record lasted just two weeks: Brazil's Neymar scored a goal after just 15 seconds against Honduras in the Semifinals.

From the Beckie record breaker, Canada went on to win their opener 2-0 over Australia. Canada were reduced to 10 players in the 19th minute (Shelina Zadorsky got a red card for pulling down Michelle Heyman), but Sinclair scored her first goal of the tournament in the 80th minute. Three days later, Beckie scored another two and Sinclair got her second of the tournament as Canada won 3-1 over Zimbabwe.

"It is expected now, we never have any doubt that (Sinclair) will come out and perform for us," said Beckie. "I am still amazed and in awe of the player that she is and the person that she is. We know who she is on and off the field; I look up to her and the rest of the team looks up to her. It was just another day at the office for her, which is really exciting because I think it's still nowhere close to where she can be."

Canada against the Olympic champions Germany

Germany have long had one of the most successful women's football programs in the world. Before 2016, they won two FIFA World Cups, one

BACK-TO-BACK BRONZE MEDALS

FIFA World Cup Silver Medal, three Olympic Bronze Medals, and eight European Championships.

Germany faced Canada for the first time in 1994 at Montréal and went on to win all 12 matches in a 20-year period through 2014. Canada were outscored 39-12 in those first 12 matches against Germany, but by the 11th and 12th matches coach Herdman had reduced the deficit to one-goal losses at Paderborn in 2013 and at Vancouver in 2014.

At the Rio 2016 Olympic Games, Canada had already secured their spot in the Quarterfinals by the time they faced Germany in the group finale for first place. While Herdman decided to rest his two goalscorers - Beckie and Sinclair - the team wasn't ready to take a back seat to the world's number-two ranked Germany. Up front, they deployed Melissa Tancredi as captain, Josée Bélanger up from her right back position, and 17-year old Deanne Rose in her first Olympic start.

Down 1-0 after 13 minutes on a Melanie Behringer penalty, Tancredi sparked the turnaround with a goal in each half as Canada beat the German powerhouse for the first time in their program's history.

"It's a great day," said Herdman after the win. "We have had a couple of great days here. The first game against Australia was one of my proudest moments as a coach to see the resilience. Today just topped it, to see the inspirational performance from our captain Tancredi."

Tancredi scored the first goal from the top of the box in the 25th minute after a pass from Desiree Scott, then scored the second goal on a header in the 60th minute on Quinn's long free kick.

"She spoke before the game," said Herdman. "She got them clear on what this game was about (as) it was about making history in a couple of ways: beating Germany for the first time and finishing top of the group with nine points. It will be very difficult for a Canadian team to ever go and match that."

Unfortunately, Germany showed just how strong of a nation they were when they beat Canada a week later in the Olympic Semifinals. Behringer again scored the first goal, but this time Sara Däbritz doubled the lead in the 59th minute and Canada just couldn't find a response. Another three days on, Germany added their first Olympic Gold Medal to their showcase after a 2-1 win over Sweden.

Canada win back-to-back Bronze Medals

By the time Canada faced the hosts Brazil in the Olympic Bronze Medal match, they had won four of their five matches with eight goals scored. In beating Brazil in their last match, Canada Soccer's Women's National Team became the first Canadian team in more than 100 years to reach the podium in back-to-back Summer Olympic Games.

Sinclair almost opened the scoring on a free kick in the ninth minute, but her near-perfect kick over the five-player wall hit the crossbar instead of the netting. Then just over 15 minutes later, 17-year old winger Rose scored on a cross from Ashley Lawrence to make it 1-0.

Early in the second half, Sinclair scored the match winner after teens Jessie Fleming and Rose combined to get the Sinclair the ball. Sinclair, as accurate as ever from about seven yards out, controlled Rose's pass and put the ball past Bárbara.

With just over 10 minutes to go, Bia Zaneratto scored Brazil's lone goal on a left-footed shot that beat Stephanie Labbé. It wasn't enough as Canada held out for the 2-1 victory at São Paulo.

"I am just super proud, not just of our team, but of every member on our staff," said Sinclair. "It has been four years of hard work, four years of dedication. We set a goal to achieve back-to-back podiums and we weren't going to settle for anything less than that. I am just super proud."

Against the odds, Canada were the only women's program in the world to reach the Olympic podium at both London 2012 and Rio 2016. They had done so by beating three confederation champions including the hosts Brazil in their own backyard.

"It was pretty surreal the whole experience," said Herdman. "The crowd was fantastic. There was just an inner belief that it was going to happen today. These girls were very clear in what they wanted to do. It has just been a great experience, this whole tournament has been fantastic."

GREATEST OF ALL TIME

SINCLAIR WINS AN OLYMPIC GOLD MEDAL

TOKYO OLYMPIC GAMES
YOKOHAMA, JAPAN
FRIDAY 6 AUGUST 2021
YOKOHAMA STADIUM

Sinclair wins an Olympic Gold Medal

With more international goals than anyone else on the planet, Christine Sinclair doesn't always have to score goals to help Canada win big matches. So while Sinclair didn't score in the Olympic Final at Tokyo in 2021, it was just her being her usual dangerous self that led to Canada scoring their 1-1 equaliser in the Final against Sweden.

In the second half, Sinclair was tripped in the penalty area, the referee called the foul, and Sinclair handed the ball to teammate Jessie Fleming who made no mistake in putting Canada level with Sweden after 67 minutes at the Yokohama Stadium.

By the time the Olympic Final reached extra time and then kicks from the penalty mark, Sinclair the veteran was cheering from the bench. She had done her job for 86 minutes and now her teammates were primed to do the rest. So Fleming scored on Canada's first kick, Deanne Rose scored in between a couple of big saves by Stephanie Labbé, and Julia Grosso scored on the last kick to win Canada their first Olympic Gold Medal.

Tokyo Olympic Games in 2021

Canada went undefeated across the Tokyo Olympic Games in 2021 as they successfully "changed the colour of their (Olympic) Medal" from Bronze to Gold. It was the third Olympic Games in which Canada climbed the podium, albeit the first time accompanied by the playing of their national anthem. For captain Sinclair, still only 38 years young, it was a most-deserved first Olympic Gold Medal for the world's all-time international goalscoring leader.

Sinclair scored in the opening 1-1 draw with hosts Japan, then Canada won 2-1 over Chile and drew 1-1 with Great Britain. After they beat Brazil 4-3 on kicks in the Olympic Quarterfinals, they beat USA 1-0 in the Olympic Semifinals, their first victory over the Americans in 20 years. Canada then got the better of the Swedes in the Olympic Gold Medal Final with a 3-2 win on kicks.

In light of the global pandemic, the Olympic Committee introduced "flexibility for team rosters" which meant that for the first time each team's 22 selected players were all part of the Olympic roster (instead of just 18 players until an injury forced a change to the roster). Teams were also allowed to make five substitutions in each match (instead of three), with a sixth substitution permitted in the case of extra time. With the new rules in place, Head Coach Bev Priestman featured 21 different players with only Janine Beckie, Kadeisha Buchanan and Ashley Lawrence starters in all six matches. By the time Canada reached the knockout phase, Priestman featured the same 11 starters from the Quarterfinals through to the Gold Medal Final.

Stadium, referees and lineups

YOKOHAMA, JAPAN - Friday 6 August 2021 at Yokohama Stadium. **REFEREES** - Anastasia Pustovoitova (RUS); Ekaterina Kurochkina (RUS); Sanja Rodak (CRO); Salima Mukansanga (RWA). **VIDEO ASSISTANT REFEREES** - Bibiana Steinhaus-Webb (GER); Marco Guida (ITA).
CANADA - 1 GK Stephanie Labbé; 10 Ashley Lawrence, 14 Vanessa Gilles, 3 Kadeisha Buchanan, 2 Allysha Chapman (8 Jayde Riviere 93'), 11 Desiree Scott (4 Shelina Zadorsky 120'), 5 Quinn (7 Julia Grosso 46'), 17 Jessie Fleming, 12 Christine Sinclair captain (19 Jordyn Huitema 86'), 16 Janine Beckie (9 Adriana Leon 46'), 15 Nichelle Prince (6 Deanne Rose). Head coach: Bev Priestman. Did not feature: 18 GK Kailen Sheridan. Alternates: 22 GK Erin McLeod, 13 Evelyne Viens, 20 Sophie Schmidt, 21 Gabrielle Carle.
SWEDEN - 1 GK Hedvig Lindahl; 4 Hanna Glas, 13 Amanda Ilestedt (3 Emma Kullberg 120'), 14 Nathalie Björn, 6 Magdalena Eriksson (2 Jonna Andersson 75'), 17 Caroline Seger captain, 18 Fridolina Rolfö (15 Olivia Schough 106'), 10 Sofia Jakobsson (5 Hanna Bennison 75'), 16 Filippa Angeldal (8 Lina Hurtig 75'), 11 Stina Blackstenius (19 Anna Anvegård 106'), 9 Kosovare Asllani. Head coach: Peter Gerhardsson. Did not feature: 12 GK Jennifer Falk. Alternates: 22 GK Zećira Mušović; 7 Madelen Janogy, 20 Julia Roddar, 21 Rebecka Blomqvist.

Canada qualify for the Olympic Games

It was a different world when Canada qualified for the Olympic Games in February 2020. At the Concacaf Olympic Qualifiers that year, Sinclair set the world's all-time international goalscoring record in Edinburg, Texas, then Canada qualified for the Olympic Games in Carson, California. In the Concacaf Final, Canada lost 3-0 to their rivals USA in front of 17,489 fans at Carson's Health Dignity Park near Los Angeles.

After Canada won all three of their group matches in Texas, they then qualified for the Olympic Games with a 1-0 win over Costa Rica. Sinclair scored three goals across the group phase including the match winner in an important 2-0 victory over Mexico to help them avoid the Americans in the Concacaf Semifinals. Jordyn Huitema, who like Julia Grosso and Jayde Riviere wasn't even born when Sinclair started playing international football, scored the match winner to qualify Canada for the Olympic Games.

"Costa Rica made it difficult, but we dominated, we finally got one, and we were so solid defensively that we weren't going to give one up after that," said Sinclair after the win. "Going to the Olympic Games never gets old and every one brings a different story and different experience. We can now look forward to getting back on that podium."

Coach Priestman takes charge of Canada

Canada were in the north of France when the world changed within the matter of a week because of the global Covid-19 pandemic. On a Wednesday, they lost 1-0 to hosts France in front of 7,054 spectators at the Stade de l'Épopée. Less than a week later in a Tuesday match at the same stadium, there were no spectators in the building as they came from behind to get a 2-2 draw against Brazil.

As it turned out, their draw against Brazil was their last international match of the year. Within a few days of the players' return to clubs in USA, England, Sweden and France, they found themselves locked in their homes with their professional seasons suspended.

While club football did return later that year, Canada's international schedule was on hold until 2021. As a result of the delay in the Olympic Games, Canada had to search for a new Head Coach because Kenneth Heiner-Møller was scheduled to return home and lead the Danish Football Union's coach education program starting in September (which was originally after the Olympic Games). Canada's new Head Coach, Bev Priestman, started in November 2020.

"I look forward to connecting with the great group of staff and players ready to head into the Olympic year of 2021 focused and ready to give it our all," said Priestman as part of Canada Soccer's announcement at the end of October.

Priestman brought some familiarity to the program as she had worked alongside Heiner-Møller as an assistant coach to John Herdman at the Rio 2016 Olympic Games. Priestman had left for England in 2018 (she was an assistant coach at the FIFA World Cup in 2019), but was now back in Canada on the road to the Olympic Games at Tokyo.

Sinclair scores in the Olympic opener

Just over two weeks before Julia Grosso scored on the last kick of the Tokyo Olympic Games, captain Sinclair got things started with the opening goal against the hosts Japan. It was Sinclair's 12th career

Olympic goal and the fourth tournament in a row that she put herself on the scoresheet. It was also her milestone 300th international "A" appearance for Canada.

It took Sinclair less than six minutes to the find the back of the net as she scored on her own rebound from the goal post. On the play, Ashley Lawrence played Nichelle Prince down the right wing, Prince crossed it to Sinclair in the box who hit the post, and then Sinclair knocked it in with her left foot from inside the six-yard box.

"It was great to get ahead early and I thought we played well to start the game," said Sinclair. "It's a shame we couldn't hold on to the three points, but we'll take the point and move on."

Canada beat America in the Olympic Semifinals

After their opening draw against Japan, Canada won 2-1 over Chile on a pair of goals by Janine Beckie. Three days later, they took a 1-0 lead over Great Britain on an Adriana Leon goal in the 55th minute, but had to settle for a 1-1 draw after a Caroline Weir shot deflected off Nichelle Prince in the 85th minute. With the draw, Great Britain won the group while Canada finished in second place, but Canada were content to qualify for the Quarterfinals undefeated through three matches.

CANADIAN LEGEND • JESSIE FLEMING

Jessie Fleming scored in back-to-back matches at the Olympic Games in 2021, both the 1-0 winner over USA in the Semifinals and the 1-1 equaliser in the Gold Medal Final against Sweden. Against Sweden, she was the first of three Canadians to score on kicks from the penalty mark as Canada captured the Gold Medal.

Fleming has already won back-to-back Olympic medals and represented Canada at back-to-back FIFA World Cups. She was Canada's joint top goalscorer in 2021 and 2022 and won her fourth Concacaf Silver Medal in 2022.

Since 2013, Fleming and Sinclair have been on the pitch together more than 100 times for Canada. While Sinclair is a 14-time winner of Canada Soccer's Player of the Year award, Fleming has already won the prize in 2021 and 2022. At the club level, they faced each other for the first time at the 2022 Women's International Champions Cup when Fleming's Chelsea FC beat Portland Thorns FC for third place.

"We are undefeated in three matches and we've put ourselves in control of our own destiny," said goalkeeper Labbé, who returned to action after an injury in the opening match. "We know our ultimate goal and we're on our way to that goal."

In the Olympic Quarterfinals, neither Labbé nor her Brazilian opponent Bárbara were beaten after 120 minutes of play, although Vanessa Gilles did hit the crossbar on a header just before the hour mark. On kicks from the penalty mark, Bárbara stopped Sinclair's initial kick, then Marta put Brazil ahead 1-0. Jessie Fleming, Débinha, Ashley Lawrence, Érika and Adriana Leon all took turns beating the goalkeeper, but then Labbé stopped Andressa on the eighth kick to keep the score tied 3-3. Gilles made it 4-3 and Labbé saved Rafaelle's attempt for the win.

Canada were through to the Olympic Semifinals and, just about three hours later, so too were the Americans.

"I am really proud of the resilient performance that the group put in," said coach Priestman. "They went right to the very end and I've said all tournament that big players step up in big moments. I had no doubt in my mind in that moment that the penalty was going to be saved (by Labbé). Just over the moon: a really great Canadian performance and Canadian moment."

It was difficult for Canadians not to think back to the London 2012 Olympic Semifinals ahead of the 2021 clash at Kashima. After all, that 2012 match was an emotional roller coaster that caught the attention of the world and the ire of a nation.

While the two sides knew each other so well, the Canadians had now gone 20 years without a victory over the Americans. In their nine meetings since the London 2012 Olympic Games, Canada managed two draws and even kept a couple of their losses to just one goal, but it was still seven losses in nine matches against the Americans.

On this night at Kashima, however, there was just no turning back the Canadians as they won 1-0 on a penalty goal by the unflappable Fleming in the 74th minute. Deanne Rose drew the penalty after she was taken down in the box by centre back Tierna Davidson.

Like it would happen in the Final, the Video Assistant Referee Pawel Raczkowski alerted the Referee Kateryna Monzul. After Monzul's review, the penalty was called. Fleming then powered her right-footed penalty past the diving substitute goalkeeper Adrianna Franch for the 1-0 Canada lead. For the next 20 nervy minutes (including four minutes of added time), Canadians around the world held their collective breath, crossed their fingers, prayed to the football gods, and wished for the final whistle.

Finally, Monzul called the match and Canada were through to their first Olympic Final.

"Our goal heading here was to change the colour of the Medal after back-to-back Bronze Medals," said Sinclair. "What a performance, what a fight, I'm just so proud of our team and (we've got) one more to go.

"For those of us who were part of 2012, it was nice to get a little revenge in an Olympic Semifinals," continued Sinclair. "This is a very unique and special group, one I'm very proud to be part of (because) we fight for everything.

"Job one is done for us, changing the colour of the Medal, but now that we're in the Final, we go for it. This tournament is grueling, that's why I'm proud that we have 22 players strong that can step on the field and make a difference and (so far) they have (in) this tournament."

Olympic Gold Medal Final

Canada were a resolute group and, while they were happy to have changed the colour of their Olympic Medal, they weren't about to settle for anything less than Gold. In the Olympic Final, Canada faced a mighty good team in Sweden, the Olympic Silver Medal winners from Rio 2016 and third-place finishers from the recent FIFA World Cup in 2019. Like Canada, Sweden were aiming for their first world title.

"I've never played an Olympic Final before, but I've played in a lot of big games and I think that helps," said Sinclair after the Final. "I just wanted to help this team win, whatever was needed, whether that was clearing corners in our (six-yard box), I don't care, I just want to help the team win. I don't think I did anything special tonight, I just did my job. We have such a great group. Everyone stepped up, everyone did their job, that's what made it unique."

After Stina Blackstenius scored the opener in the first half, Fleming got the equaliser in the second half. This time, it was Video Assistant Referee Bibiana Steinhaus-Webb who notified Referee Anastasia Pustovoitova of the potential foul in the penalty area. Pustovoitova watched the replay and agreed: Amanda Ilestedt fouled Sinclair to the ground with her left leg inside the box while Sinclair was awaiting the incoming cross from Allysha Chapman.

It took more than two minutes to make the call, but once confirmed, Sinclair picked up the ball and handed it to cool-as-a-cucumber Fleming for the penalty kick. Fleming made no mistake with her kick and the two sides were level in the Gold Medal Final.

Another 23-plus minutes went by, then another 30 minutes of extra time, but neither side could beat the goalkeepers. Fans watching from around the world were on the edge of their seats for the first-ever Olympic Gold Medal Final to be decided by kicks from the penalty mark.

It was a wild and thrilling ending.

"I am so glad we won, but for a tournament to come down to PK's, in a way it is a coin toss to be honest," said Sinclair a few days later. "I think it was the first shootout that I have ever actually not physically been a part of where I am on the sidelines and it was the worst experience of my life. I wish people had a camera on Desiree Scott and I throughout the course of that shootout because we were absolutely going insane and having heart attacks and going through everything.

"But as a team, we had been together for over 40 days and at every single practice we worked on our PK's knowing that a lot of tournaments come down to them. Very rarely do you see a team win a tournament without at some point, whether it is in game or in a shootout, advancing with the help of PK's. So we worked on them and had extreme trust in ourselves and then we had Steph Labbé in goal who was like a brick wall and insane.

"So we liked our chances, but it is so stressful and, uh, I can't, yeah, I can't even describe what we were going through."

The best team won the Olympic Games

Canada were unbeaten across six matches in Japan as they became Canada Soccer's first National Teams side to win a major world title (FIFA World Cup or Olympic Games). Labbé was of course the star of the last match as she became the first Canadian goalkeeper to twice make two saves on kicks from the penalty mark in the same competition (Quarterfinals and Gold Medal Final).

"I honestly cannot believe what just happened for the last 40 days," said Sinclair. "We had a goal coming here to change the colour of the Medal and we landed on the top of the podium. It's just such an honour to be part of this group, it's such a special group. We fought through the whole tournament, we fought tonight and managed to find a way to win."

Next to Sinclair in the press conference, coach Priestman agreed.

"I think we knew and we said we will start strong and finish strong and that's the (Olympic) Games, that's the tournament (and) we grew through the tournament. The more moments you get, the bigger the belief. I think tonight's Gold Medal win epitomizes this group: they fought until the very, very end. They weren't willing to let that slip and that's a testament to all the players.

"I think the young players coming through tonight stepped up and delivered. I think Christine hit the nail on the head (when she spoke), I think it's a very special group, it's a great blend and they managed to do it. They wanted to do whatever it took to make their country proud and they've absolutely done that."

Back home a few days later, Sinclair explained further.

"I will tell you that there is no greater feeling than standing on the top of the podium with your best friends, with the people that you've experienced all the joys and all the lows that sport brings you. Standing up there, listening to the Canadian national anthem, it is a moment I will never forget.

"Heading into every tournament, we've known that our x-factor is always our connection. I think a lot of teams say that they are a close-knit team, but we truly are. These are some of my best friends and they have been for years and we have been through a lot together. Throughout the course of the tournament, we choose to spend time together, we choose to play games and that's how we pass the time.

"I think what you saw in this tournament was that the best team won. All that Bev asked of us was that each player just do their part, no one had to play out of their minds. She knew that we had the components to go far in this tournament and everyone just needed to do their job and you saw that through the course of the entire tournament. The same goes to the staff, just everyone did their job, we put it all together, and somehow managed to win a Gold Medal."

GREATEST OF ALL TIME

185

THE GREATEST GOALSCORER OF ALL TIME

CHRISTINE SINCLAIR, O.C.
OLYMPIC CHAMPION
PROFESSIONAL FOOTBALL CHAMPION
WORLD RECORD HOLDER

The greatest goalscorer of all time is Canadian

The world's all-time international goalscoring record belongs to Christine Sinclair and she's not done yet. As we pulled this book together, Sinclair herself was preparing for her sixth FIFA World Cup in the Summer of 2023. For the first time, Canada were entering a FIFA or Olympic event as the number-one team to beat, the reigning Olympic champions from the summer of 2021.

The record books will tell you that Sinclair has scored 190 international "A" goals for Canada across her first 23 seasons. She officially set the record during the 2020 Concacaf Olympic Qualifiers in Edinburg, Texas, poetically the tournament that qualified Canada for the Olympic Games in which they won their Gold Medal a year later.

"I am a very proud Canadian," said Sinclair in 2020. "When I first joined the National Team, I had goals, dreams and aspirations of passing Mia Hamm one day. I should have aimed higher, not knowing that Abby Wambach would have beaten her, but I never could have imagined reaching the totals that I have. For all who have supported me through my career, a massive thank you."

The Wolfpack

190 Christine Sinclair
184 Abby Wambach
158 Mia Hamm

"Mia Hamm, who grew up playing when professional women's soccer didn't even exist, achieved the record for most international goals scored in the world," wrote Abby Wambach after Sinclair broke her record. "She was my mentor, my friend, she was the leader of our Pack.

"In June 2013, I scored the goal to pass my hero's record. For the six and a half years that I've held the world record - by man or woman - I've been grateful-to-the-bones for the path the Pack before me tread so that I could spend my life playing the game I love. I've tried to live and play in a way honouring that legacy and privilege, so that little girls coming up after us will accomplish things we've only dreamed of.

"So, as a girl who grew up dreaming of winning Olympic Gold for my country before women's soccer was even an Olympic sport, tonight I am celebrating. Tonight I am celebrating the honour of passing that record, that legacy of our beautiful game, to the great Christine Sinclair: world-record holder for most international goals - man or woman - in history.

"Christine: history is made. Your victory is our victory. We celebrate with you.

THE WOLFPACK • ABBY WAMBACH

An honoured member of the U.S. Soccer Hall of Fame, Abby Wambach is a FIFA World Cup champion (2015), FIFA World Cup runner up (2011), and two-time Olympic Gold Medal winner (2004, 2012). At the club level, she was a WUSA Founder's Cup winner with the Washington Freedom and an NWSL Shield winner with the Western New York Flash.

From 2001 to 2015, she scored a world-record 184 international "A" goals in 255 matches, a record only passed by Christine Sinclair in 2020. Wambach was also a six-time U.S. Soccer Athlete of the Year and one-time FIFA World Player of the Year.

With USA, Wambach scored 10 goals in 22 career matches against Canada, including two goals at Vancouver in the 2012 Concacaf Olympic Qualifiers Final.

"To every girl coming up in the Pack with a dream to do something that doesn't yet even exist: we believe in you to accomplish what we can't even yet imagine. Your Pack is with you. And history awaits you."

World international goalscoring record

Christine Sinclair became the world's all-time international goalscoring leader after she scored a pair of goals in the opening match of her 21st season on 29 January 2020. She scored both of her goals in the first half of an 11-0 win over St. Kitts and Nevis, with the opener scored on a penalty in the seventh minute and the record breaker scored in the 23rd minute on a right-footed shot from less than eight yards out.

On the historic play, Jessie Fleming won the turnover on the right and pressed forward to attack, she played it into the box for Adriana Leon who then quickly one-timed her pass to Sinclair. The Canada captain steadied the ball before she slipped her shot past the goalkeeper Kyra Dickinson for the world record.

The World congratulates Sinclair

After Sinclair's historic goal, social media channels like Facebook, Instagram and Twitter were flooded with countless messages of admiration from teammates, opponents, coaches, administrators, fans, and dignitaries including the Governor General of Canada Julie Payette and the Prime Minister of Canada Justin Trudeau. The Governor General wrote "bravo for being such an inspiration" while the Prime Minister wrote "Congratulations, you rock!"

From the world's governing body, FIFA President Gianni Infantino wrote, "this achievement rewards your outstanding 20-year career at the highest level, which could only be achieved thanks to your tremendous commitment, exemplary motivation, hard work and incredible passion for our beautiful game. Your human qualities and skills, not to mention your remarkable contribution to the popularity and growth of women's football, or soccer, deserve our admiration."

From the regional confederation in which Canada plays, Concacaf President and fellow British Columbian Victor Montagliani wrote, "Christine's achievements have made her an icon in Canada. She transcends the sport and is a wonderful role model for people across the country. I hope she continues leading the line for the National Team and scoring goals. I thank her for the enormous contribution she has made to the sport in Canada, the Concacaf region and across the world."

Said Canada Soccer President Steven Reed, also from British Columbia, "Christine Sinclair is the greatest international goalscorer in the world's most beloved sport. We have watched her grow from teenage star on the local grounds to international superstar who is adored around the world. For more than 20 years, she has served as a global ambassador to our nation, continually raising the bar for our sport through her achievements on the pitch and her humble actions off the pitch."

Canada's Athlete of the Year

In 2020, Sinclair won the Bobbie Rosenfeld Award as *The Canadian Press* Female Athlete of the Year for the second time. She was the first team-sport athlete to win the Rosenfeld award twice (2012 and 2020).

From 2002 to 2020, Sinclair was an eight-time top-five finalist in voting for the Rosenfeld Award. At 19 years, it marked the longest era by a Canadian team-sport athlete ranked in the top-five voting for *The Canadian Press* Athlete of the Year awards. Only golfers Marlene Stewart-Streit (35 years), Ada MacKenzie (21) and Stan Leonard (20) were recognised in the top-five across longer eras.

By comparison, hockey's Maurice "Rocket" Richard was a seven-time top-five finalist across 13 years in voting for the men's Lionel Conacher Award, Jean Béliveau was a four-time top-five finalist across 14 years, Wayne Gretzky was a 13-time top-five finalist across 15 years, and Mario Lemieux was an 11-time top-five finalist across 17 years.

"Christine Sinclair, an absolute treasure to Canada and Canadian sport, is truly deserving of her remarkable achievement in setting the world's all-time international goalscoring record," said Peter Montopoli, Canada Soccer's General Secretary in 2020. "She has been making history throughout her career, leading Canada with skill, determination, pride and honour on the international stage. There is only one Christine Sinclair and she is simply the greatest of all time."

Alongside Sinclair as the Female Athlete of the Year in 2020, Canadian footballer Alphonso Davies was *The Canadian Press* Male Athlete of the Year in the same year. With Davies and Sinclair, the duo were just the fifth pair of athletes from the same sport to win *The Canadian Press*

Athlete of the Year awards in the same year (athletics 1936, golf 2000, ice hockey 2007, and tennis 2013 and 2014).

Christine Sinclair's Canada teammates

Across Sinclair's first 185 international goals, there were 96 different teammates on the pitch in those moments when she scored for Canada.

Midfielder Diana Matheson was the lone player on the pitch for more than a century of those goals, 105 to be exact. Matheson was sidelined with an injury when Sinclair scored her record-breaking goal at Edinburg in 2020, but she was otherwise in action for 82 different matches in which Sinclair scored at least one goal between 2003 and 2019.

Most matches on the pitch when Christine Sinclair scored:
105 Diana Matheson
87 Rhian Wilkinson
81 Sophie Schmidt
75 Candace Chapman
74 Randee Hermus
65 Karina LeBlanc
63 Erin McLeod
58 Desiree Scott
53 Melissa Tancredi
50 Brittany Timko

WORLD-RECORD HOLDER • KRISTINE LILLY

An honoured member of the U.S. Soccer Hall of Fame, Kristine Lilly is a FIFA World Cup champion (1999), a two-time Olympic Gold Medal winner (1996, 2004), and one-time Olympic Silver Medal winner (2000). At the club level, she helped the Boston Breakers win one WUSA regular-season title.

From 1987 to 2010, Lilly scored 130 goals in a world-record 354 international "A" appearances for the United States. She retired ranked second in the world in goals behind only teammate Mia Hamm. She was also a two-time U.S. Soccer Athlete of the Year.

With USA, Lilly scored 12 goals in 31 career matches against Canada, in fact the most matches ever played by an opponent against Canada. She notably scored against Canada in the 1991 Concacaf Championship Final, the 2003 FIFA World Cup Match for 3rd Place, and the 2006 Concacaf Gold Cup Final (the match winner in added time of extra time).

On Tuesday 14 March 2000, Sinclair scored her first international goal in Canada's second match at the Algarve Cup in Albufeira, Portugal. It was a 2-1 loss to Norway, but Sinclair scored the opening goal against Bente Nordby in the eighth minute of the match. At the time, she was the youngest goalscorer in the history of the women's program (she was also the youngest debutant just two days earlier at age 16).

On that day in 2000, Head Coach Even Pellerud's starting lineup against his former team featured Nicole Wright (goal), Breanna Boyd, Tanya Franck, Andrea Neil, Sharolta Nonen, Cindy Walsh, Shannon Rosenow, Isabelle Harvey, Randee Hermus, captain Amy Walsh and goalscorer Sinclair.

Goals by competition, by opponent, by situation

Christine Sinclair was most dominant scoring goals against Concacaf opponents, but she was also very deadly in FIFA World Cups as well as Olympic competitions. With two goals against St. Kitts and Nevis, she improved her all-time record to 44 goals in 40 Concacaf matches (2000 to 2020). On the world stage, she scored 10 goals in 21 FIFA World Cup matches (2003 to 2019) and 11 goals in her first 15 Olympic matches (2008 to 2016).

Her two goals against St. Kitts and Nevis were also the first two goals she ever scored against that opponent. From her first 185 international goals, she scored most often against Mexico (16 goals), China PR (12 goals) and Jamaica, Costa Rica and USA (11 goals against each). At the time, she had scored against 42 different nations at the international "A" level (she added Nigeria to her list in April 2022 when she scored her 189th career goal).

From her first 185 goals, more than 85% of them put Canada ahead on the scoresheet: she scored 78 goals that put Canada ahead by one (the go-ahead goal) and 80 goals that extended Canada's lead by two or more. In the 99 wins in which she scored a goal, she scored the match winner 59 times (in all, she had played in 156 wins for Canada). With Canada trailing, she scored the tying goal 15 times and she closed the gap in the score 12 times.

To dig a little deeper or to have a little fun, we can tell you that she scored most often on a Saturday (41 times), most often in the month of March (37 times), and equally often in either the first or last 15 minutes of the second half.

"The goals... that's something that has happened over the course of a very long career," said Olympic champion Sinclair in 2021. "For me, I've just always just been able to score goals. Give me a chance and most of the time I am able to put it in the back of the net. It's something that my parents even said I was able to do when I was like five years old learning how to play, they would say 'you always just knew how to score.'

"In the past in my career I put pressure on myself, playing for the National Team knowing I had to score goals to help the team be successful. As our team has gotten better and deeper, I know that I just need to play well and do anything I can to help the team win. I don't need to put extra pressure on myself to score goals, we now have other people that can put the ball in the back of the net, so it has been very freeing these past few years to just take that pressure off myself and to just be able to play. I think with (the Olympic) tournament you saw we have a number of goalscorers, people that will put the ball in the back of the net and that's a big relief for me."

The Best FIFA Special Award

In January 2022, Christine Sinclair was presented The Best FIFA Special Award for her lifetime achievement of scoring more international goals than any other player in the history of the game. It was a truly deserving honour for a special player that had worn Canada's colours since she was 16 years old at the start of the millennium.

"I have never played this sport for the goals, I have never played this sport for the individual awards, I have actually never played this sport for the team awards either," said Sinclair in 2022. "I just love this sport, I love the concept of it, I love figuring out with your teammates how to exploit weaknesses of opponents, how to use your strengths... it fascinates me. I discovered soccer at a very young age and I was passionate about it. You couldn't get a soccer ball away from me since I was like four.

"This (award) is something that I am sure when my career is done I will look back on this recognition and be like, this was pretty cool. It just goes to show (the growth) that our National Team has made, our program has made, the growth of the NWSL and the growth of women's football. To be honoured as the first (recipient of this award) makes it that much more special."

Sinclair wasn't able to travel to Zurich for The Best FIFA Awards in early 2022, which at the time was a virtual event on account of the global pandemic. She accepted the award from Portland as part of a live broadcast for the award winners (Sinclair's Portland teammates surprised her by joining her at a closed event in Portland).

"I would like to take this time to thank FIFA for this once-in-a-lifetime recognition," said Sinclair to FIFA President Gianni Infantino. "First and foremost, I'd like to thank my family for their support and guidance throughout my entire career. From my parents' constant support and allowing their little girl to leave home at a young age to chase my dreams, to my brother for tolerating his younger sister for all those years. I hope he knows all I wanted to be was him. I'm standing here today because of all of you.

"Throughout my career I've been fortunate to experience many successes, from winning trophies internationally and at club level and accepting individual awards. But, honestly, the victories are quickly forgotten... except winning that Olympic Gold Medal – I'll remember that one forever.

"But what truly matters most is the moments I've shared and the connections I've made. From celebrating with an entire country to experiencing the heartbreak of defeat with those closest to me. To all my teammates and staff members along the way, I hope you know how thankful I am for all of you. Together, we've had the ultimate goal of inspiring generations and changing the sport in our country. And I tell you, we've accomplished that and more.

"At this point in my career, the thing I'm most proud of is being able to have been a part of the game from the very beginning, where there was limited support, limited professional environments, to now, where it's truly a global game, where there's professional environments, successful leagues, successful international tournaments.

"I do want to say that women's football, women, female athletes have often been an afterthought. My goal moving forward is to continue the fight, continue the change and to continue growing the sport we all love."

THE GREATEST GOALSCORER

185

CHRISTINE SINCLAIR GOALS RECORD

CHRISTINE SINCLAIR, O.C.
OLYMPIC CHAMPION
PROFESSIONAL FOOTBALL CHAMPION
WORLD RECORD HOLDER

Youth International Goals

MATCH DAY	LOCATION	COMPETITION	CANADA		SCORE	
Wed. 2001-07-25	Gjorvik, NOR	Nordic Cup	U-21	D	1:1	NOR
Sun. 2001-07-29	Kapp, NOR	Nordic Cup	U-21	W	2:1	FIN
Sun. 2001-07-29	Kapp, NOR	Nordic Cup	U-21	W	2:1	FIN
Tue. 2001-07-31	Kapp, NOR	Nordic Cup	U-21	W	6:2	ISL
Tue. 2001-07-31	Kapp, NOR	Nordic Cup	U-21	W	6:2	ISL
Sun. 2002-06-02	Vaughan, ON, CAN	U-19 Friendly	U-19	W	3:1	ITA
Tue. 2002-06-04	Oshawa, ON, CAN	U-19 Friendly	U-19	W	5:0	ITA
Wed. 2002-07-03	Ch'town, PE, CAN	U-19 Friendly	U-19	W	4:0	MEX
Fri. 2002-07-05	Wolfville, NS, CAN	U-19 Friendly	U-19	W	7:2	MEX
Fri. 2002-07-05	Wolfville, NS, CAN	U-19 Friendly	U-19	W	7:2	MEX
Fri. 2002-07-05	Wolfville, NS, CAN	U-19 Friendly	U-19	W	7:2	MEX
Fri. 2002-07-05	Wolfville, NS, CAN	U-19 Friendly	U-19	W	7:2	MEX
Sun. 2002-07-28	Victoria, BC, CAN	U-19 Friendly	U-19	W	9:1	TPE
Sun. 2002-07-28	Victoria, BC, CAN	U-19 Friendly	U-19	W	9:1	TPE
Wed. 2002-07-31	Burnaby, BC, CAN	U-19 Friendly	U-19	W	11:0	TPE
Wed. 2002-07-31	Burnaby, BC, CAN	U-19 Friendly	U-19	W	11:0	TPE
Wed. 2002-07-31	Burnaby, BC, CAN	U-19 Friendly	U-19	W	11:0	TPE
Sun. 2002-08-18	Edmonton, AB, CAN	FIFA U-19 World's	U-19	W	3:2	DEN
Tue. 2002-08-20	Edmonton, AB, CAN	FIFA U-19 World's	U-19	W	4:0	JPN
Tue. 2002-08-20	Edmonton, AB, CAN	FIFA U-19 World's	U-19	W	4:0	JPN
Thu. 2002-08-22	Edmonton, AB, CAN	FIFA U-19 World's	U-19	W	2:0	NGA
Thu. 2002-08-22	Edmonton, AB, CAN	FIFA U-19 World's	U-19	W	2:0	NGA
Sun. 2002-08-25	Edmonton, AB, CAN	FIFA U-19 World's	U-19	W	6:2	ENG
Sun. 2002-08-25	Edmonton, AB, CAN	FIFA U-19 World's	U-19	W	6:2	ENG
Sun. 2002-08-25	Edmonton, AB, CAN	FIFA U-19 World's	U-19	W	6:2	ENG
Sun. 2002-08-25	Edmonton, AB, CAN	FIFA U-19 World's	U-19	W	6:2	ENG
Sun. 2002-08-25	Edmonton, AB, CAN	FIFA U-19 World's	U-19	W	6:2	ENG

Christine Sinclair Goals Record

2000 International Season

MATCH DAY	LOCATION	COMPETITION	CANADA		SCORE	
Tue. 2000-03-14	Albufeira, POR	Algarve Cup	CAN	L	1:2	NOR
Sat. 2000-03-18	Lagos, POR	Algarve Cup	CAN	W	3:2	DEN
Sat. 2000-03-18	Lagos, POR	Algarve Cup	CAN	W	3:2	DEN
Wed. 2000-05-31	Canberra, AUS	Pacific Cup	CAN	W	2:1	NZL
Fri. 2000-06-02	Sydney, AUS	Pacific Cup	CAN	L	1:9	USA
Sun. 2000-06-04	Campbelltown, AUS	Pacific Cup	CAN	W	2:0	AUS
Thu. 2000-06-08	Newcastle, AUS	Pacific Cup	CAN	D	2:2	CHN
Thu. 2000-06-08	Newcastle, AUS	Pacific Cup	CAN	D	2:2	CHN
Sat. 2000-06-10	Newcastle, AUS	Pacific Cup	CAN	W	5:1	JPN
Sat. 2000-06-24	Foxborough, MA, USA	CONCACAF Gold Cup	CAN	W	4:3	MEX
Sat. 2000-06-24	Foxborough, MA, USA	CONCACAF Gold Cup	CAN	W	4:3	MEX
Wed. 2000-06-28	Louisville, KY, USA	CONCACAF Gold Cup	CAN	W	12:0	GUA
Wed. 2000-06-28	Louisville, KY, USA	CONCACAF Gold Cup	CAN	W	12:0	GUA
Wed. 2000-06-28	Louisville, KY, USA	CONCACAF Gold Cup	CAN	W	12:0	GUA
Sat. 2000-11-11	Columbus, OH, USA	International Friendly	CAN	W	3:1	USA

CHRISTINE SINCLAIR GOALS RECORD

2001 & 2002 youth (28 goals)

BROADCAST	GOAL, DISTANCE, FINAL TOUCH & ASSIST					STADIA (ATT.)
	2	1-1				Raufoss
	1	1-0				Fauchald
	3	2-1				Fauchald
	1	1-0				Fauchald
	2	2-0				Fauchald
						Dufferin District Park
	4	4-0				Civic
	3	3-0				MacAdam Field (2,600)
	1	1-0				Acadia U. (3,600)
	2	2-0				Acadia U. (3,600)
	4	3-1				Acadia U. (3,600)
	6	5-1				Acadia U. (3,600)
	1	1-0				UVic Centennial
	4	3-1				UVic Centennial
	2	2-0				Swangard (5,581)
	5	5-0				Swangard (5,581)
	6	6-0				Swangard (5,581)
FIFA, Sportsnet	1	1-0		Header from play	Lang	Commonwealth (25,000)
FIFA, Sportsnet	1	1-0		Right foot	Andrews	Commonwealth (15,714)
FIFA, Sportsnet	2	2-0		Left foot	Chapman	Commonwealth (15,714)
FIFA, Sportsnet	1	1-0	PK	PK Right foot	-	Commonwealth (15,803)
FIFA, Sportsnet	2	2-0		Header from CK	Booth	Commonwealth (15,803)
FIFA, Sportsnet	1	1-0	<6y	Header from CK	Moscato	Commonwealth (23,595)
FIFA, Sportsnet	2	2-0	<18y	Right foot	Moscato	Commonwealth (23,595)
FIFA, Sportsnet	4	4-0	<6y	Left foot		Commonwealth (23,595)
FIFA, Sportsnet	7	5-2	<18y	Right foot		Commonwealth (23,595)
FIFA, Sportsnet	8	6-2	<18y	Left foot	-	Commonwealth (23,595)

LEGEND: <6y = Inside the 6-yard box; <18y = Inside the 18...; >>>> = Outside the 18...

2000 CANWNT (15 goals)

BROADCAST	GOAL, DISTANCE, FINAL TOUCH & ASSIST					STADIA (ATT.)
	1	1-0				Municipal de Albufeira (200)
	1	1-0				Municipal de Lagos
	4	3-1				Municipal de Lagos
	3	2-1				AIS Athletics
	10	1-9			Latham	Sydney (10,049)
	1	1-0			Morneau	Campbelltown
	1	1-0				Breakers
	2	2-0				Breakers
	1	1-0				Hunter Athletics
Sportsnet	2	1-1	<18y	Left foot		Foxboro (6,223)
Sportsnet	5	3-2	<6y	Header from play	-	Foxboro (6,223)
Sportsnet	1	1-0	<18y	Right foot	Bowie	Cardinal (3,048)
Sportsnet	8	8-0	>>>>	Right foot	Walsh	Cardinal (3,048)
Sportsnet	9	9-0	<6y	Left foot	Hooper	Cardinal (3,048)
ESPN2	1	1-0	>>>>	Left foot	Hooper	Crew (8,569)

2001 International Season

MATCH DAY		LOCATION	COMPETITION	CANADA SCORE			
Sat.	2001-02-10	Rabat, MAR	International Friendly	CAN	W	4:0	MAR
Sun.	2001-03-11	Lagos, POR	Algarve Cup	CAN	W	3:0	USA
Tue.	2001-03-13	Silves, POR	Algarve Cup	CAN	L	2:5	SWE
Tue.	2001-03-13	Silves, POR	Algarve Cup	CAN	L	2:5	SWE
Sat.	2001-03-17	Loulé, Faro, POR	Algarve Cup	CAN	L	1:5	CHN
Sat.	2001-06-30	Toronto, ON, CAN	International Friendly	CAN	D	2:2	USA

2002 International Season

MATCH DAY		LOCATION	COMPETITION	CANADA SCORE			
Sun.	2002-03-03	Lagoa, POR	Algarve Cup	CAN	W	4:0	WAL
Sun.	2002-03-03	Lagoa, POR	Algarve Cup	CAN	W	4:0	WAL
Tue.	2002-03-05	Silves, POR	Algarve Cup	CAN	W	7:1	POR
Tue.	2002-03-05	Silves, POR	Algarve Cup	CAN	W	7:1	POR
Wed.	2002-10-30	Victoria, BC, CAN	Concacaf Gold Cup	CAN	W	11:1	HAI
Wed.	2002-10-30	Victoria, BC, CAN	Concacaf Gold Cup	CAN	W	11:1	HAI
Wed.	2002-10-30	Victoria, BC, CAN	Concacaf Gold Cup	CAN	W	11:1	HAI
Wed.	2002-10-30	Victoria, BC, CAN	Concacaf Gold Cup	CAN	W	11:1	HAI
Fri.	2002-11-01	Victoria, BC, CAN	Concacaf Gold Cup	CAN	W	9:0	JAM
Fri.	2002-11-01	Victoria, BC, CAN	Concacaf Gold Cup	CAN	W	9:0	JAM
Sun.	2002-11-03	Victoria, BC, CAN	Concacaf Gold Cup	CAN	W	3:0	CRC

2003 International Season

MATCH DAY		LOCATION	COMPETITION	CANADA SCORE			
Thu.	2003-03-20	Guia, POR	Algarve Cup	CAN	W	7:1	GRE
Thu.	2003-03-20	Guia, POR	Algarve Cup	CAN	W	7:1	GRE
Thu.	2003-03-20	Guia, POR	Algarve Cup	CAN	W	7:1	GRE
Sat.	2003-04-26	Washington, DC, USA	International Friendly	CAN	L	1:6	USA
Thu.	2003-06-12	Guasave, SI, MEX	International Friendly	CAN	W	4:0	MEX
Sun.	2003-06-15	Mazatlán, SI, MEX	International Friendly	CAN	W	2:1	MEX
Sat.	2003-08-16	Seattle, WA, USA	International Friendly	CAN	D	1:1	GHA
Sun.	2003-08-31	Edmonton, AB, CAN	International Friendly	CAN	W	8:0	MEX
Sat.	2003-09-20	Columbus, OH, USA	FIFA World Cup	CAN	L	1:4	GER
Sat.	2003-09-27	Foxborough, MA, USA	FIFA World Cup	CAN	W	3:1	JPN
Sat.	2003-10-11	Carson, CA, USA	FIFA World Cup	CAN	L	1:3	USA

2004 International Season

MATCH DAY		LOCATION	COMPETITION	CANADA SCORE			
Sun.	2004-02-01	Shenzhen, CHN	Four Nations Tourney	CAN	L	1:3	SWE
Thu.	2004-02-26	Herédia, CRC	Concacaf Oly. Qualifiers	CAN	W	6:0	JAM
Thu.	2004-02-26	Herédia, CRC	Concacaf Oly. Qualifiers	CAN	W	6:0	JAM
Thu.	2004-02-26	Herédia, CRC	Concacaf Oly. Qualifiers	CAN	W	6:0	JAM
Fri.	2004-03-05	Herédia, CRC	Concacaf Oly. Qualifiers	CAN	W	4:0	CRC
Fri.	2004-03-05	Herédia, CRC	Concacaf Oly. Qualifiers	CAN	W	4:0	CRC

CHRISTINE SINCLAIR GOALS RECORD

2001 CANWNT (15 goals)

BROADCAST	GOAL, DISTANCE, FINAL TOUCH & ASSIST				STADIA (ATT.)
	2	2-0			
	2	2-0		Kiss	Municipal de Lagos (150)
	4	1-3		Walsh	Dr. Francisco Vieira
	6	2-4		Hermus	Dr. Francisco Vieira
	1	1-0			
Sportsnet	4	2-2	<18y Right foot	-	Varsity (9,023)

2002 CANWNT (11 goals)

BROADCAST	GOAL, DISTANCE, FINAL TOUCH & ASSIST				STADIA (ATT.)
	1	1-0			Capitão Josino Costa
	3	3-0			Capitão Josino Costa
	3	3-0			Dr. Francisco Vieira
	8	7-1			Dr. Francisco Vieira
Sportsnet	4	3-1	<18y Right foot	-	UVic Centennial (1,531)
Sportsnet	8	7-1	<18y Left foot	-	UVic Centennial (1,531)
Sportsnet	9	8-1	<6y Right foot	Chapman	UVic Centennial (1,531)
Sportsnet	12	11-1	<6y Left foot	Boyd	UVic Centennial (1,531)
Sportsnet	1	1-0	<18y Right foot	Hooper	UVic Centennial (1,834)
Sportsnet	7	7-0	<18y Right foot	Kiss	UVic Centennial (1,834)
Sportsnet	3	3-0	<6y Header from CK	Burtini	UVic Centennial (3,256)

2003 CANWNT (11 goals)

BROADCAST	GOAL, DISTANCE, FINAL TOUCH & ASSIST				STADIA (ATT.)
	1	1-0	<6y Right foot	Neil	Arsénio Catuna
	3	3-0	<18y Header from play		Arsénio Catuna
	7	7-0	<18y Right foot	Hooper	Arsénio Catuna
ESPN2	1	1-0	>>>> Right foot	Booth	RFK Stadium (5,693)
	1	1-0			Armando Leyson
	2	1-1			(2,123)
	1	1-0			Memorial (5)
Sportsnet	4	4-0		Latham	Commonwealth (29,953)
FIFA	1	1-0	<18y Header from FK	Kiss	Crew (16,409)
FIFA	3	2-1	<6y Header from CK	Timko	Gillette (14,356)
FIFA	2	1-1	<18y Right foot	Latham	Home Depot (25,253)

2004 CANWNT (6 goals)

BROADCAST	GOAL, DISTANCE, FINAL TOUCH & ASSIST				STADIA (ATT.)
	4	1-3		-	Shenzhen
Sportsnet	3	3-0	Left foot	Matheson	Rosabal Cordero (3,000)
Sportsnet	4	4-0			Rosabal Cordero (3,000)
Sportsnet	6	6-0		Hermus	Rosabal Cordero (3,000)
Sportsnet	1	1-0			Rosabal Cordero (2,004)
Sportsnet	4	4-0			Rosabal Cordero (2,004)

2005 International Season

MATCH DAY	LOCATION	COMPETITION	CANADA SCORE
Sun. 2005-04-24	Hildesheim, GER	International Friendly	CAN L 2:3 GER
Wed. 2005-05-25	København, DEN	International Friendly	CAN W 4:3 DEN
Wed. 2005-05-25	København, DEN	International Friendly	CAN W 4:3 DEN
Sat. 2005-05-28	Stockholm, SWE	International Friendly	CAN L 1:3 SWE

2006 International Season

MATCH DAY	LOCATION	COMPETITION	CANADA SCORE
Thu. 2006-02-23	Mexicali, BC, MEX	International Friendly	CAN W 3:1 MEX
Thu. 2006-02-23	Mexicali, BC, MEX	International Friendly	CAN W 3:1 MEX
Tue. 2006-07-18	Blaine, MN, USA	International Friendly	CAN W 4:2 SWE
Sat. 2006-08-26	Rouen, FRA	International Friendly	CAN W 1:0 FRA
Tue. 2006-08-29	St-Aubin-sur-Scie, FRA	International Friendly	CAN D 2:2 FRA
Sat. 2006-10-28	Seoul, KOR	Peace Queen Cup	CAN W 3:2 ITA
Sat. 2006-10-28	Seoul, KOR	Peace Queen Cup	CAN W 3:2 ITA
Mon. 2006-10-30	Masan, KOR	Peace Queen Cup	CAN W 3:1 KOR
Mon. 2006-10-30	Masan, KOR	Peace Queen Cup	CAN W 3:1 KOR
Mon. 2006-10-30	Masan, KOR	Peace Queen Cup	CAN W 3:1 KOR
Wed. 2006-11-01	Changwon, KOR	Peace Queen Cup	CAN W 4:2 BRA
Wed. 2006-11-22	Carson, CA, USA	Concacaf Gold Cup	CAN W 4:0 JAM
Wed. 2006-11-22	Carson, CA, USA	Concacaf Gold Cup	CAN W 4:0 JAM

2007 International Season

MATCH DAY	LOCATION	COMPETITION	CANADA SCORE
Thu. 2007-05-03	Nanjing, CHN	International Friendly	CAN L 1:3 CHN
Sat. 2007-05-12	Frisco, TX, USA	International Friendly	CAN L 2:6 USA
Sun. 2007-06-03	Auckland, NZL	International Friendly	CAN W 3:0 NZL
Sun. 2007-06-03	Auckland, NZL	International Friendly	CAN W 3:0 NZL
Wed. 2007-06-06	Auckland, NZL	International Friendly	CAN W 5:0 NZL
Sat. 2007-07-14	Rio, BRA	Pan American Games	CAN W 7:0 URU
Sat. 2007-07-14	Rio, BRA	Pan American Games	CAN W 7:0 URU
Sat. 2007-07-14	Rio, BRA	Pan American Games	CAN W 7:0 URU
Wed. 2007-07-18	Rio, BRA	Pan American Games	CAN W 11:1 JAM
Wed. 2007-07-18	Rio, BRA	Pan American Games	CAN W 11:1 JAM
Wed. 2007-07-18	Rio, BRA	Pan American Games	CAN W 11:1 JAM
Wed. 2007-07-18	Rio, BRA	Pan American Games	CAN W 11:1 JAM
Thu. 2007-07-26	Rio, BRA	Pan American Games	CAN W 2:1 MEX
Sat. 2007-09-15	Hangzhou, CHN	FIFA World Cup	CAN W 4:0 GHA
Sat. 2007-09-15	Hangzhou, CHN	FIFA World Cup	CAN W 4:0 GHA
Thu. 2007-09-20	Chengdu, CHN	FIFA World Cup	CAN D 2:2 AUS

2008 International Season

MATCH DAY	LOCATION	COMPETITION	CANADA SCORE
Fri. 2008-03-07	Larnaka, CYP	Cyprus Cup	CAN W 3:0 JPN
Fri. 2008-03-07	Larnaka, CYP	Cyprus Cup	CAN W 3:0 JPN
Fri. 2008-03-07	Larnaka, CYP	Cyprus Cup	CAN W 3:0 JPN
Wed. 2008-04-02	Juárez, CH, MEX	Concacaf Oly. Qualifiers	CAN W 6:0 TRI
Sat. 2008-06-14	Suwon, KOR	Peace Queen Cup	CAN W 5:0 ARG
Sat. 2008-06-14	Suwon, KOR	Peace Queen Cup	CAN W 5:0 ARG

CHRISTINE SINCLAIR GOALS RECORD

2005 CANWNT (4 goals)

BROADCAST	GOAL, DISTANCE, FINAL TOUCH & ASSIST				STADIA (ATT.)
	5	2-3			Sportanlage MTV (8,000)
	4	1-3			Rasunda (1,513)
	7	4-3		Hooper	Rasunda (1,513)
	4	1-3		Neil	National Arena (2,503)

2006 CANWNT (13 goals)

BROADCAST	GOAL, DISTANCE, FINAL TOUCH & ASSIST				STADIA (ATT.)
	1	1-0			Necaxa
	3	3-0			Necaxa
	4	3-1		Timko	National Sports (2,206)
	1	1-0			Robert-Diochon (1,260)
	2	1-1	PK	-	des Vertus (1,558)
	1	1-0			Seoul World Cup
	2	2-0			Seoul World Cup
	1	1-0			Masan
	3	2-1			Masan
	4	3-1			Masan
	4	3-1		Wilkinson	Changwon Civil
Sportsnet	1	1-0	<18y	Left foot	Home Depot (6,128)
Sportsnet	3	3-0	<18y	Right foot	-	Home Depot (6,128)

2007 CANWNT (16 goals)

BROADCAST	GOAL, DISTANCE, FINAL TOUCH & ASSIST				STADIA (ATT.)
	1	1-0			Nanjing Sports Center
(TV)	6	2-4	<18y	Right foot	Walsh	Toyota (8,569)
	1	1-0			North Harbour (2,500)
	3	3-0			North Harbour (2,500)
	2	2-0		Kiss	North Harbour
	1	1-0		Thorlakson	Miécimo de Silva
	4	4-0			Miécimo de Silva
	6	6-0			Miécimo de Silva
	1	1-0			Zico Centre
	2	2-0			Zico Centre
	4	4-0			Zico Centre
	7	7-0			Zico Centre
	1	1-0			Maracanã
FIFA, CBC, etal	1	1-0	<6y	Header from play	Lang	Dragon (33,835)
FIFA, CBC, etal	3	3-0	<18y	Right foot	Lang	Dragon (33,835)
FIFA, CBC, etal	3	2-1	<6y	Header from play	Chapman	Chengdu (29,300)

2008 CANWNT (13 goals)

BROADCAST	GOAL, DISTANCE, FINAL TOUCH & ASSIST				STADIA (ATT.)
	1	1-0	PK	-	GSZ
	2	2-0		Wilkinson	GSZ
	3	3-0		Matheson	GSZ
CBC	6	6-0			Benito Juarez (7,000)
(TV)	2	2-0	<18y	Right foot	-	Worldcup (26,370)
(TV)	3	3-0	<18y	Header from play	Tancredi	Worldcup (26,370)

MATCH DAY	LOCATION	COMPETITION	CANADA SCORE
Mon. 2008-06-16	Suwon, KOR	Peace Queen Cup	CAN W 3:1 KOR
Mon. 2008-06-16	Suwon, KOR	Peace Queen Cup	CAN W 3:1 KOR
Wed. 2008-06-18	Suwon, KOR	Peace Queen Cup	CAN W 2:0 NZL
Thu. 2008-07-10	Toronto, ON, CAN	International Friendly	CAN D 1:1 BRA
Sat. 2008-07-26	Singapore, SIN	International Friendly	CAN D 1:1 NZL
Sat. 2008-08-09	Tianjin, CHN	Olympic Tournament	CAN D 1:1 CHN
Fri. 2008-08-15	Shanghai, CHN	Olympic Tournament	CAN L 1:2 USA

2009 International Season

MATCH DAY	LOCATION	COMPETITION	CANADA SCORE
Sat. 2009-03-07	Larnaka, CYP	Cyprus Cup	CAN W 2:1 NED
Sat. 2009-03-07	Larnaka, CYP	Cyprus Cup	CAN W 2:1 NED
Tue. 2009-03-10	Larnaka, CYP	Cyprus Cup	CAN W 2:0 RUS
Thu. 2009-03-12	Nicosia, CYP	Cyprus Cup	CAN L 1:3 ENG

2010 International Season

MATCH DAY	LOCATION	COMPETITION	CANADA SCORE
Sat. 2010-02-20	Larnaka, CYP	International Friendly	CAN W 3:0 POL
Wed. 2010-02-24	Larnaka, CYP	Cyprus Cup	CAN W 2:1 SUI
Thu. 2010-09-30	Toronto, ON, CAN	International Friendly	CAN W 3:1 CHN
Sun. 2010-10-31	Cancún, QR, MEX	Concacaf Championship	CAN W 8:0 GUY
Sun. 2010-10-31	Cancún, QR, MEX	Concacaf Championship	CAN W 8:0 GUY
Sun. 2010-10-31	Cancún, QR, MEX	Concacaf Championship	CAN W 8:0 GUY
Sun. 2010-10-31	Cancún, QR, MEX	Concacaf Championship	CAN W 8:0 GUY
Fri. 2010-11-05	Cancún, QR, MEX	Concacaf Championship	CAN W 4:0 CRC
Mon. 2010-11-08	Cancún, QR, MEX	Concacaf Championship	CAN W 1:0 MEX
Thu. 2010-12-09	São Paulo, BRA	II Torneio Internacional	CAN W 5:0 NED
Thu. 2010-12-09	São Paulo, BRA	II Torneio Internacional	CAN W 5:0 NED
Sun. 2010-12-12	São Paulo, BRA	II Torneio Internacional	CAN W 1:0 MEX
Sun. 2010-12-19	São Paulo, BRA	II Torneio Internacional	CAN D 2:2 BRA

2011 International Season

MATCH DAY	LOCATION	COMPETITION	CANADA SCORE
Fri. 2011-01-21	Yongchuan, CHN	Yongchuan Cup	CAN W 3:2 CHN
Fri. 2011-01-21	Yongchuan, CHN	Yongchuan Cup	CAN W 3:2 CHN
Tue. 2011-01-25	Yongchuan, CHN	Yongchuan Cup	CAN W 1:0 SWE
Mon. 2011-03-07	Nicosia, CYP	Cyprus Cup	CAN W 2:0 ENG
Sun. 2011-06-26	Berlin, GER	FIFA World Cup	CAN L 1:2 GER
Tue. 2011-10-18	Guadalajara, JA, MEX	Pan American Games	CAN W 3:1 CRC
Thu. 2011-10-27	Guadalajara, JA, MEX	Pan American Games	CAN D 1:1 BRA
Tue. 2011-11-22	Phoenix, AZ, USA	International Friendly	CAN W 2:1 SWE

2012 International Season

MATCH DAY	LOCATION	COMPETITION	CANADA SCORE
Thu. 2012-01-19	Vancouver, BC, CAN	Concacaf Oly. Qualifiers	CAN W 6:0 HAI
Thu. 2012-01-19	Vancouver, BC, CAN	Concacaf Oly. Qualifiers	CAN W 6:0 HAI
Thu. 2012-01-19	Vancouver, BC, CAN	Concacaf Oly. Qualifiers	CAN W 6:0 HAI
Thu. 2012-01-19	Vancouver, BC, CAN	Concacaf Oly. Qualifiers	CAN W 6:0 HAI
Sat. 2012-01-21	Vancouver, BC, CAN	Concacaf Oly. Qualifiers	CAN W 2:0 CUB

CHRISTINE SINCLAIR GOALS RECORD

BROADCAST	GOAL, DISTANCE, FINAL TOUCH & ASSIST				STADIA (ATT.)
(TV)	2	2-0	>>>>	Right foot	Matheson	Worldcup (1,224)
(TV)	3	3-0	>>>>	Right foot	-	Worldcup (1,224
(TV)	1	1-0	>>>>	Left foot	Tancredi	Worldcup
Sportsnet	1	1-0	<18y	Right foot	Rustad	BMO Field (13,554
	1	1-0				Queenston
CBC Sports	1	1-0	<18y	Right foot	Lang	Tianjin (52,600)
CBC Sports	2	1-1	>>>>	Right foot	Rustad	Shanghai (26,129)

2009 CANWNT (4 goals)

BROADCAST	GOAL, DISTANCE, FINAL TOUCH & ASSIST				STADIA (ATT.)
-	1	1-0	<18y	Right foot	Julien	GSZ (25)
-	2	2-0	<18y	Right foot	Wilkinson	GSZ (25)
-	1	1-0	>>>>	Right foot	Matheson	Ammochostos (25)
-	1	1-0	>>>>	Left foot	Tancredi	GSP (50)

2010 CANWNT (13 goals)

BROADCAST	GOAL, DISTANCE, FINAL TOUCH & ASSIST				STADIA (ATT.)
-	1	1-0	<18y	Left foot	-	Alpha Sports (30)
-	2	1-1	PK	PK Right foot	-	Ammochostos (75)
Sportsnet	4	3-1	<18y	Left foot	Bélanger	BMO Field (5,427)
CBC etal	2	2-0	<18y	Right foot	-	Beto Ávila (482)
CBC, etal	4	4-0	<6y	Right foot	Chapman	Beto Ávila (482)
CBC, etal	5	5-0	<18y	Left foot	Filigno	Beto Ávila (482)
CBC, etal	6	6-0	>>>>	Left foot	-	Beto Ávila (482)
CBC, etal	3	3-0	<6y	Left foot	-	Beto Ávila (2,000)
CBC, etal	1	1-0	PK	PK Right foot	-	Quintana Roo (16,005)
Band Sports	1	1-0	>>>>	Left foot	Kyle	Pacaembu (3,397)
Band Sports	5	5-0	<18y	Left foot	-	Pacaembu (3,397)
Band Sports	1	1-0	<18y	Left foot	Tancredi	Pacaembu (7,681)
Band Sports	4	2-2	>>>>	Left foot	-	Pacaembu (17,264)

2011 CANWNT (8 goals)

BROADCAST	GOAL, DISTANCE, FINAL TOUCH & ASSIST				STADIA (ATT.)
CCTV	4	2-2	<18y	Left foot	Tancredi	Sports Center (10,000)
CCTV	5	3-2	<18y	Right foot	Tancredi	Sports Center (10,000)
CCTV Sports	1	1-0	>>>>	Left foot	Zurrer	Sports Center (12,000)
-	1	1-0	<6y	Left foot	-	GSP (30)
FIFA, CBC, etal	3	1-2	>>>>	FK Right foot	-	Olympiastadion (73,680)
Terra Deportes	3	2-1			Kyle	Omnilife (4,000)
Terra Deportes	2	1-1	<18y	Header from CK	Matheson	Omnilife (10,000)
	3	2-1	<6y	Body	Zurrer	Grand Canyon (50)

2012 CANWNT (23 goals)

BROADCAST	GOAL, DISTANCE, FINAL TOUCH & ASSIST				STADIA (ATT.)
Sportsnet etal	2	2-0	<18y	Right foot	Wilkinson	BC Place (7,627)
Sportsnet etal	3	3-0	<18y	Left foot	Julien	BC Place (7,627)
Sportsnet etal	4	4-0	<18y	Left foot	Tancredi	BC Place (7,627)
Sportsnet etal	5	5-0	PK	PK Right foot	-	BC Place (7,627)
Sportsnet etal	1	1-0	PK	PK Right foot	-	BC Place (12,417)

MATCH DAY	LOCATION	COMPETITION	CANADA SCORE			
Mon. 2012-01-23	Vancouver, BC, CAN	Concacaf Oly. Qualifiers	CAN	W	5:1	CRC
Mon. 2012-01-23	Vancouver, BC, CAN	Concacaf Oly. Qualifiers	CAN	W	5:1	CRC
Fri. 2012-01-27	Vancouver, BC, CAN	Concacaf Oly. Qualifiers	CAN	W	3:1	MEX
Fri. 2012-01-27	Vancouver, BC, CAN	Concacaf Oly. Qualifiers	CAN	W	3:1	MEX
Tue. 2012-02-28	Larnaka, CYP	Cyprus Cup	CAN	W	5:1	SCO
Thu. 2012-03-01	Nicosia, CYP	Cyprus Cup	CAN	W	2:1	ITA
Sat. 2012-03-24	Foxborough, MA, USA	International Friendly	CAN	W	2:1	BRA
Sat. 2012-03-24	Foxborough, MA, USA	International Friendly	CAN	W	2:1	BRA
Wed. 2012-05-30	Moncton, NB, CAN	International Friendly	CAN	W	1:0	CHN
Mon. 2012-07-09	Vevey, SUI	International Friendly	CAN	W	1:0	COL
Sat. 2012-07-14	Châtel-Saint-Denis, SUI	Match world Cup	CAN	W	2:0	NZL
Tue. 2012-07-17	Savièse, SUI	Match world Cup	CAN	L	1:2	BRA
Sat. 2012-07-28	Coventry, ENG	Olympic Tournament	CAN	W	3:0	RSA
Sat. 2012-07-28	Coventry, ENG	Olympic Tournament	CAN	W	3:0	RSA
Fri. 2012-08-03	Coventry, ENG	Olympic Tournament	CAN	W	2:0	GBR
Mon. 2012-08-06	Manchester, ENG	Olympic Tournament	CAN	L	3:4	USA
Mon. 2012-08-06	Manchester, ENG	Olympic Tournament	CAN	L	3:4	USA
Mon. 2012-08-06	Manchester, ENG	Olympic Tournament	CAN	L	3:4	USA

2013 International Season

MATCH DAY	LOCATION	COMPETITION	CANADA SCORE			
Fri. 2013-03-08	Nicosia, CYP	Cyprus Cup	CAN	W	2:1	FIN
Mon. 2013-03-11	Nicosia, CYP	Cyprus Cup	CAN	W	1:0	NED
Wed. 2013-10-30	Edmonton, AB, CAN	International Friendly	CAN	W	3:0	KOR
Thu. 2013-12-12	Brasilia, BRA	Torneio Internacional	CAN	W	2:0	SCO

2014 International Season

MATCH DAY	LOCATION	COMPETITION	CANADA SCORE			
Wed. 2014-11-26	Los Angeles, CA, USA	International Friendly	CAN	D	1:1	SWE

2015 International Season

MATCH DAY	LOCATION	COMPETITION	CANADA SCORE			
Tue. 2015-01-13	Shenzhen, CHN	International Friendly	CAN	W	2:1	MEX
Thu. 2015-01-15	Shenzhen, CHN	International Friendly	CAN	W	2:1	CHN
Thu. 2015-01-15	Shenzhen, CHN	International Friendly	CAN	W	2:1	CHN
Wed. 2015-03-04	Nicosia, CYP	Cyprus Cup	CAN	W	2:0	SCO
Fri. 2015-03-06	Larnaka, CYP	Cyprus Cup	CAN	W	1:0	KOR
Sat. 2015-06-06	Edmonton, AB, CAN	FIFA World Cup	CAN	W	1:0	CHN
Sat. 2015-06-27	Vancouver, BC, CAN	FIFA World Cup	CAN	L	1:2	ENG
Wed. 2015-12-09	Natal, BRA	Torneio Internacional	CAN	W	3:0	MEX
Wed. 2015-12-09	Natal, BRA	Torneio Internacional	CAN	W	3:0	MEX
Sun. 2015-12-13	Natal, BRA	Torneio Internacional	CAN	W	4:0	TRI

2016 International Season

MATCH DAY	LOCATION	COMPETITION	CANADA SCORE			
Sun. 2016-02-14	Houston, TX, USA	Concacaf Oly. Qualifiers	CAN	W	6:0	TRI
Fri. 2016-02-19	Houston, TX, USA	Concacaf Oly. Qualifiers	CAN	W	3:1	CRC
Fri. 2016-02-19	Houston, TX, USA	Concacaf Oly. Qualifiers	CAN	W	3:1	CRC
Sun. 2016-04-10	Eindhoven, NED	International Friendly	CAN	W	2:1	NED

CHRISTINE SINCLAIR GOALS RECORD

BROADCAST	GOAL, DISTANCE, FINAL TOUCH & ASSIST				STADIA (ATT.)
Sportsnet etal	1	1-0	<6y	Left foot	Booth	BC Place (8,105)
Sportsnet etal	4	4-0	<18y	Right foot	Wilkinson	BC Place (8,105)
Sportsnet etal	1	1-0	<18y	Left foot	Tancredi	BC Place (22,954)
Sportsnet etal	4	3-1	>>>>	Right foot	Tancredi	BC Place (22,954)
	5	4-1			-	GSZ (25)
-	1	1-0			Woeller	GSP (30)
	1	1-0	<18y	Left foot	Chapman	Gillette (3,000)
	2	2-0	<18y	Left foot	Schmidt	Gillette (3,000)
Sportsnet	1	1-0	<18y	Left foot	Matheson	Moncton (7,514)
-	1	1-0			Sesselmann	de Copet (50)
EuroWorld Sport	2	2-0			Schmidt	de Lussy (1,500)
EuroWorld Sport	2	1-1			-	St-Germain (2,000)
CTV Olympics	2	2-0	<18y	Header from play	Sesselmann	Coventry (14,753)
CTV Olympics	3	3-0	<18y	Right foot	Schmidt	Coventry (14,753)
CTV Olympics	2	2-0	>>>>	FK Right foot	-	Coventry (28,828)
CTV Olympics	1	1-0	<18y	Right foot	Tancredi	Old Trafford (26,630)
CTV Olympics	3	2-1	<18y	Header from play	Tancredi	Old Trafford (26,630)
CTV Olympics	5	3-2	<18y	Header from CK	Schmidt	Old Trafford (26,630)

2013 CANWNT (4 goals)

BROADCAST	GOAL, DISTANCE, FINAL TOUCH & ASSIST				STADIA (ATT.)
-	3	1-2	PK	PK Right foot	-	GSP (50)
-	1	1-0	>>>>	Right foot	Filigno	GSP (50)
Sportsnet One	1	1-0	<6y	Header from CK	Matheson	Commonwealth (12,746)
Band Sports	2	2-0	<18y	Left foot	-	Garrincha (400)

2014 CANWNT (one goal)

BROADCAST	GOAL, DISTANCE, FINAL TOUCH & ASSIST				STADIA (ATT.)
-	2	1-1	<18y	Right foot	Iacchelli	Drake (30)

2015 CANWNT (10 goals)

BROADCAST	GOAL, DISTANCE, FINAL TOUCH & ASSIST				STADIA (ATT.)
-	3	2-1	<6y	Right foot	-	Bao'an (532)
CCTV-5	2	1-1	PK	PK Right foot	-	Bao'an (6,683)
CCTV-5	3	2-1	<18y	Right foot	Scott	Bao'an (6,683)
-	2	2-0	>>>>	Right foot	Wilkinson	GSP Nicosia (30)
-	1	1-0	<18y	Right foot	-	GSZ (30)
FIFA, TSN etal	1	1-0	PK	PK Right foot	-	Commonwealth (53,058)
FIFA, TSN etal	3	1-2	<6y	Left foot	-	BC Place (54,027)
Band Sports	1	1-0	<18y	Right foot	Buchanan	Dunas (500)
Band Sports	2	2-0	<18y	Right foot	Wilkinson	Dunas (500)
Band Sports	4	4-0	<18y	Left foot	Bélanger	Dunas (6,428)

2016 CANWNT (7 goals)

BROADCAST	GOAL, DISTANCE, FINAL TOUCH & ASSIST				STADIA (ATT.)
CBCSports.ca	3	3-0	<18y	Right foot	Beckie	BBVA (1,453)
Sportsnet etal	1	1-0	<18y	Right foot	Bélanger	BBVA (5,516)
Sportsnet etal	2	2-0	<18y	Left foot	-	BBVA (5,516)
Fox NL, TSN Go	1	1-0	<18y	Right foot	Beckie	Jan Louwers (2,122)

MATCH DAY	LOCATION	COMPETITION	CANADA SCORE
Wed. 2016-08-03	São Paulo, BRA	Olympic Tournament	CAN W 2:0 AUS
Sat. 2016-08-06	São Paulo, BRA	Olympic Tournament	CAN W 3:1 ZIM
Fri. 2016-08-19	São Paulo, BRA	Olympic Tournament	CAN W 2:1 BRA

2017 International Season

MATCH DAY	LOCATION	COMPETITION	CANADA SCORE
Wed. 2017-03-01	Lagos, POR	Algarve Cup	CAN W 1:0 DEN
Fri. 2017-03-03	São João da Venda, POR	Algarve Cup	CAN W 2:1 RUS
Thu. 2017-06-08	Winnipeg, MB, CAN	International Friendly	CAN W 3:1 CRC
Tue. 2017-11-28	Marbella, ESP	International Friendly	CAN W 3:2 NOR

2018 International Season

MATCH DAY	LOCATION	COMPETITION	CANADA SCORE
Fri. 2018-03-02	São João da Venda, POR	Algarve Cup	CAN W 1:0 RUS
Mon. 2018-03-05	Lagos, POR	Algarve Cup	CAN W 3:0 KOR
Mon. 2018-03-05	Lagos, POR	Algarve Cup	CAN W 3:0 KOR
Sun. 2018-06-10	Hamilton, ON, CAN	International Friendly	CAN L 2:3 GER
Mon. 2018-10-08	Edinburg, TX, USA	Concacaf Championship	CAN W 12:0 CUB
Thu. 2018-10-11	Edinburg, TX, USA	Concacaf Championship	CAN W 3:1 CRC
Sun. 2018-10-14	Frisco, TX, USA	Concacaf Championship	CAN W 7:0 PAN
Sun. 2018-10-14	Frisco, TX, USA	Concacaf Championship	CAN W 7:0 PAN

2019 International Season

MATCH DAY	LOCATION	COMPETITION	CANADA SCORE
Tue. 2019-01-22	La Manga, ESP	International Friendly	CAN W 1:0 NOR
Fri. 2019-03-01	Lagos, POR	Algarve Cup	CAN W 1:0 SCO
Fri. 2019-04-05	Manchester, ENG	International Friendly	CAN W 1:0 ENG
Sat. 2019-05-18	Toronto, ON, CAN	International Friendly	CAN W 3:0 MEX
Thu. 2019-06-20	Reims, FRA	FIFA World Cup	CAN L 1:2 NED
Sun. 2019-11-10	Yongchuan, CHN	International Friendly	CAN W 3:0 NZL

2020 International Season

MATCH DAY	LOCATION	COMPETITION	CANADA SCORE
Wed. 2020-01-29	Edinburg, TX, USA	Concacaf Oly. Qualifiers	CAN W 11:0 SKN
Wed. 2020-01-29	Edinburg, TX, USA	Concacaf Oly. Qualifiers	CAN W 11:0 SKN
Tue. 2020-02-04	Edinburg, TX, USA	Concacaf Oly. Qualifiers	CAN W 2:0 MEX

2021 International Season

MATCH DAY	LOCATION	COMPETITION	CANADA SCORE
Wed. 2021-07-21	Sapporo, JPN	Olympic Tournament	CAN D 1:1 JPN
Sat. 2021-10-23	Ottawa, ON, CAN	Celebration Tour	CAN W 5:1 NZL

2022 International Season

MATCH DAY	LOCATION	COMPETITION	CANADA SCORE
Mon. 2022-04-11	Victoria, BC, CAN	International Friendly	CAN D 2:2 NGA
Tue. 2022-07-05	Guadalupe, NL, MEX	Concacaf Championship	CAN W 6:0 TRI

CHRISTINE SINCLAIR GOALS RECORD

BROADCAST	GOAL, DISTANCE, FINAL TOUCH & ASSIST					STADIA (ATT.)
CBC etal	2	2-0	>>>>	Right foot	Fleming	Corinthians (20,521)
CBC etal	2	2-0	PK	PK Right foot	-	Corinthians (30,295)
CBC etal	2	2-0	<18y	Right foot	Rose	Corinthians (39,718)

2017 CANWNT (4 goals)

BROADCAST	GOAL, DISTANCE, FINAL TOUCH & ASSIST					STADIA (ATT.)
DBU TV	1	1-0	<18y	Left foot	-	Municipal de Lagos (150)
-	2	2-0	<18y	Left foot	-	Algarve (75)
TSN, RDS2	2	2-0	PK	PK Right foot	-	Investors Group (14,434)
CanadaSoccerTV	3	1-2	<18y	Right foot	-	Marbella (150)

2018 CANWNT (8 goals)

BROADCAST	GOAL, DISTANCE, FINAL TOUCH & ASSIST					STADIA (ATT.)
-	1	1-0	PK	PK Right foot	-	Algarve (50)
-	1	1-0	<6y	Right foot	-	Municipal de Lagos
-	3	3-0	<18y	Left foot	-	Municipal de Lagos
TSN	2	1-1	<18y	Header from play	Beckie	Tim Hortons (22,826)
ConcacafGO	10	10-0	<18y	Right foot	-	H-E-B (414)
ConcacafGO	3	3-0	<18y	Left foot	Chapman	H-E-B (330)
ConcacafGO	1	1-0	<18y	Header from play	Beckie	Toyota (1,489)
ConcacafGO	3	3-0	<18y	Header from play	Prince	Toyota (1,489)

2019 CANWNT (6 goals)

BROADCAST	GOAL, DISTANCE, FINAL TOUCH & ASSIST					STADIA (ATT.)
CanadaSoccer	1	1-0	<18y	Header from play	Hellstrom	La Manga (100)
CanadaSoccer	1	1-0	PK	PK Right foot	-	Municipal de Lagos (250)
BBC	1	1-0	<6y	Right foot	-	Academy (5,682)
OneSoccer	2	2-0	<18y	Left foot	Beckie	BMO Field (19,610)
FIFA, TSN etal	2	1-1	<6y	Left foot	Lawrence	Auguste-Delaune (19,277)
-	1	1-0	<18y	Header from play	Lawrence	Olympic Sports (8,963)

2020 CANWNT (3 goals)

BROADCAST	GOAL, DISTANCE, FINAL TOUCH & ASSIST					STADIA (ATT.)
OneSoccer	1	1-0	PK	PK Right foot	-	H-E-B Park (820)
OneSoccer	4	4-0	<18y	Right foot	Leon	H-E-B Park (820)
OneSoccer	1	1-0	<18y	Right foot	Riviere	H-E-B Park (2,538)

2021 CANWNT (2 goals)

BROADCAST	GOAL, DISTANCE, FINAL TOUCH & ASSIST					STADIA ATT.
CBC	1	1-0	<6y	Left foot	-	Sapporo Dome
OneSoccer	2	2-0	<18y	Left foot	-	TD Place (16,386)

2022 CANWNT (2 goals)

BROADCAST	GOAL, DISTANCE, FINAL TOUCH & ASSIST					STADIA (ATT.)
OneSoccer	2	1-1	>>>>	Left foot	-	Starlight (5,434)
OneSoccer	1	1-0	<18y	Header from play	Lawrence	BBVA (908)

GREATEST OF ALL TIME

M.V.P.

CHRISTINE SINCLAIR HONOURS LIST

CHRISTINE SINCLAIR, O.C.
OLYMPIC CHAMPION
PROFESSIONAL FOOTBALL CHAMPION
WORLD RECORD HOLDER

Trophies and Championships

2000	Winner	BC Soccer Championship with Vancouver UBC Alumni
2001	Winner	Metro Women's Soccer League with Vancouver UBC Alumni
2002	Winner	NCAA Championship with the University of Portland
2005	Winner	NCAA Championship with the University of Portland
2006	Winner	USL W-League Championship with Vancouver Whitecaps FC
2010	Winner	WPS Championship with FC Gold Pride
2010	Gold Medal	Concacaf Championship with Canada
2011	Gold Medal	Pan American Games with Canada
2011	Winner	WPS Championship with Western New York Flash
2013	Winner	NWSL Championship with Portland Thorns FC
2016	Winner	NWSL Shield with Portland Thorns FC
2017	Winner	NWSL Championship with Portland Thorns FC
2020	Winner	NWSL Fall Series Community Shield with Portland Thorns FC
2021	Winner	NWSL Challenge Cup with Portland Thorns FC
2021	Winner	International Champions Cup with Portland Thorns FC
2021	Winner	NWSL Shield with Portland Thorns FC
2021	Gold Medal	Olympic Football Tournament with Canada
2022	Winner	NWSL Championship with Portland Thorns FC

Christine Sinclair Awards & Honours

2000	Winner	Canada Soccer Player of the Year
2002	Winner	Sport BC Senior Athlete of the Year
2004	Winner	Canada Soccer Player of the Year
2005	Winner	Canada Soccer Player of the Year
2005	Winner	Sport BC Senior Athlete of the Year
2006	Winner	Canada Soccer Player of the Year
2006	Winner	BC Soccer Adult Player of the Year
2007	Winner	Canada Soccer Player of the Year
2008	Winner	Canada Soccer Player of the Year
2009	Winner	Canada Soccer Player of the Year
2010	Winner	Canada Soccer Player of the Year
2011	Winner	Canada Soccer Player of the Year
2012	Winner	Canada Soccer Player of the Year
2012	Winner	Air Canada Athlete of the Year
2012	Winner	Bobbie Rosenfeld Award (Canadian Press Female Athlete of the Year)
2012	Winner	CBC Canada's Athlete of the Year
2012	Winner	Lou Marsh Memorial Trophy
2012	Winner	QMI Agency Canadian Female Athlete of the Year
2012	Winner	Sportsnet Athlete of the Year
2012	Winner	Yahoo! Canada Buzziest Canadian of the Year
2013	Winner	Canada Soccer Player of the Year
2014	Winner	Canada Soccer Player of the Year
2016	Winner	Canada Soccer Player of the Year
2012	Recipient	Queen Elizabeth II Diamond Jubilee Medal
2012	Team award	The Canadian Press Team of the Year
2012	Team award	QMI Agency Team of the Year
2013	Honoured	Canada's Walk of Fame
2013	Winner	espnW Impact 10
2016	Forward	Concacaf Female Best XI
2016	Team award	Postmedia Team of the Year
2017	Officer	Order of Canada
2018	Winner	Canada Soccer Player of the Year
2018	Forward	Concacaf Female Best XI
2019	Recipient	AthletesCAN True Sport Award
2019	Honoured	Women Against MS
2019	Team award	Canadian Olympic Hall of Fame

CHRISTINE SINCLAIR HONOURS LIST

2019	Honoured	Canada Soccer Player of the Decade
2020	Winner	Bobbie Rosenfeld Award (Canadian Press Female Athlete of the Year)
2021	Team award	The Canadian Press Team of the Year
2021	Team award	Postmedia Team of the Year
2021	Recipient	The Best FIFA Special Award
2022	Recipient	Order of British Columbia
2022	Recipient	Canada Soccer President's Award

More International Football Honours

2000	Début at 16	Canada Soccer Youngest Appearance Record
2000	Goal at 16	Canada Soccer Youngest Goalscorer Record
2002	Joint leader	Most goals at the Concacaf Gold Cup
2003	10 matches	Canada Soccer Record Undefeated Streak, Women's National Team
2004	Forward	Concacaf Olympic Qualifying All-Tournament Team
2006	Leader	Most goals at the Peace Queen Cup
2007	72nd goal	Canada Soccer Record Most International "A" Goals, Career
2008	Leader	Most goals at the Cyprus Cup
2008	Leader	Most goals at the Peace Queen Cup
2008	Winner	Peace Queen Cup Silver Ball
2009	Leader	Tied for most goals at the Cyprus Cup
2010	133rd match	Canada Soccer Record Most International "A" Appearances
2010-11	11 matches	Canada Soccer Record Undefeated Streak, Women's National Team
2011	Winner	Yongchuan Cup Most Valuable Player
2012	Leader	Most goals at the Concacaf Olympic Qualifiers
2012	Leader	Most goals at the Olympic Football Tournament
213	23 goals	Canada Soccer Record Most International "A" Goals, Season
2015	Winner	BaoAn Cup Most Valuable Player
2020	185th goal	World all-time international goalscoring record
2020	Top Moment	Canada Soccer Moment of the Year
2021	12 matches	Canada Soccer Record Undefeated Streak, Women's National Team

More Club, College & Youth Football Honours

1999	Winner	BC Soccer Youth Player of the Year
2000	Winner	BC Soccer Youth Player of the Year
2002	Forward	FIFA U-19 World Championship All-Star Team
2002	Winner	FIFA U-19 World Championship Golden Ball
2002	Winner	FIFA U-19 World Championship Golden Shoe
2002	Winner	Oregon's Bill Hayward Amateur Athlete of the Year
2004	Winner	NCAA M.A.C. Hermann Trophy
2005	Winner	Oregon's Bill Hayward Amateur Athlete of the Year
2005	Winner	NCAA M.A.C. Hermann Trophy
2006	Winner	Oregon's Harry Glickman Professional Athlete of the Year
2006	Winner	Honda-Broderick Cup
2006	Forward	USL W-League All-League Team
2006	Forward	USL W-League Championship All-Tournament Team
2006	Winner	USL W-League Championship Most Valuable Player
2009	Winner	WPS All-Star Game Most Valuable Player
2010	Leader	Most assists in the WPS
2010	Forward	WPS Best XI
2011	Leader	Most goals in the WPS
2011	Leader	Most assists in the WPS
2011	Forward	WPS Best XI
2011	Winner	WPS Championship Most Valuable Player
2013	Forward	NWSL Second XI
2013	Winner	Portland Thorns FC Most Valuable Player
2018	forward	NWSL Second XI
2018	Winner	Portland Thorns FC Supporters' Player of the Year

FRONT COVER PHOTO by R.SCOTT.
ALL PHOTOS CREDIT CANADA SOCCER LIBRARY. SCOTT (pages 4, 22, 28 49, 52, 66, 112, 114, 122), STAHLSCHMIDT (page 10), GEMNICH (page 18), WPS (page 40), PANINI (page 44), FRID (pages 60, 78), MEXSPORT (pages 6, 86, 94), PORCELLI (page 102), BAZYL (page 136), CYPRUS (page 36).